Vinegar & Char

Vinegar & Char

Verse from the Southern Foodways Alliance

To the tater tots —

Cheers?

EDITED BY Sandra Beasley *Sandra Beasley*

WELCOME BY John T. Edge

FOREWORD BY W. Ralph Eubanks *W. Ralph Eubanks*

ILLUSTRATIONS BY Julie Sola

*Published in Association with the
Southern Foodways Alliance, an institute
of the Center for the Study of Southern Culture
at the University of Mississippi*

The University of Georgia Press *Athens*

This publication is made possible in part through a grant from the Bradley Hale Fund for Southern Studies.

Permissions and credits appear on pages 105–8, which constitute an extension of this copyright page.

© 2018 by the University of Georgia Press
Athens, Georgia 30602
www.ugapress.org
All rights reserved
Designed by Erin Kirk New
Set in Miller Text
Printed and bound by Thomson-Shore, Inc.
The paper in this book meets the guidelines for permanence and durability of the Committee on Production Guidelines for Book Longevity of the Council on Library Resources.

Most University of Georgia Press titles are available from popular e-book vendors.

Printed in the United States of America
22   21   20   19   18   P   5   4   3   2   1

Library of Congress Cataloging-in-Publication Data pending

ISBN 9780820354293 (paperback: alk. paper)
ISBN 9780820354309 (ebook)

Contents

SECTION III

Welcome

Since our 1999 founding, the Southern Foodways Alliance has baked poetry into our aesthetic. Prompted by SFA commissions, the region's finest writers have delivered big truths in small bundles. "Mud Creek, Dreamland, Twixt-n-Tween / the cue-joints rise through smoke and glow like roadhouses on Heaven's way": With those words, the late Jake Adam York welcomed all to our 2002 barbecue symposium.

In succeeding years, Natasha Trethewey joined us twice. For a Gulf South symposium, she spoke of her Mississippi roots. In 2013, Trethewey returned as U.S. poet laureate to pay homage to York. Poet Kevin Young has spoken more often at SFA symposia than any other collaborator. After Rebecca Gayle Howell read in 2016, Young whispered that a book like *Vinegar and Char* might be an ideal SFA undertaking.

Sandra Beasley, whom we once engaged to write a suite of poems inspired by a cadre of fictional country-music restaurant entrepreneurs, delivered on Young's gambit. Here, she showcases poetry that grapples with the thorny issues troubling our region, from racism to poverty. True to the SFA's sometime irreverence, Beasley also embraces the playful counterbalance of well-turned lines and elegant elisions.

An organization focused on transformative storytelling, SFA believes in poets. Working meter and assonance, enjambment and alliteration, they make good on our promise to challenge conventions and cultivate progress. We regard their works as literary distillates. Brimming with boiled-down truths, the poems collected here offer insightful ways to apprehend this region anew.

—JOHN T. EDGE
Director
Southern Foodways Alliance

Taking My Stand   *A Foreword*

The South has long been a region that wrestles with its place in the world, so it is no surprise that Southerners often find themselves at odds about what it means to be Southern. Most notably, John Crowe Ransom and his doctrinaire band of Agrarian poets at Vanderbilt were determined to define the very idea of what it meant to be Southern when they wrote *I'll Take My Stand* in 1930. The Agrarians promoted the idea that those who live below the Mason-Dixon line "must be persuaded to look very critically at the advantages of becoming a 'new South.'" For them the notion of the South evolving beyond its antebellum origins and embracing an urbanism that would lead to a "new South" seemed heretical if not downright catastrophic. Instead the Agrarians believed the South must embrace a culture rooted in the land and reject the industrialism of the North. For the Agrarians, the South's past was a sacrament, and the only Southern past that mattered was that of the white Southern male landowner. There was no room to broaden the circle of what it meant to be Southern nor was there a desire for the sensibilities of the region to move beyond the nineteenth-century idea of itself.

Neither the South's self-referential perspective nor its competing narratives—from both inside and outside the region—are helpful in defining what the South is or what it means to be Southern. When I read the Agrarians as a student at the University of Mississippi in the 1970s, the use of the term "Southern tradition" peppered throughout their writing meant something different to me than it did to my white classmates, and it was not positive. Reading their work and being a student at a university that was bound tightly in Southern tradition made me take a stand, though not the one Mr. Ransom intended his readers to take. Instead, I turned my back on the South, until a midlife identity crisis led me to embrace the place of my birth on my own terms.

Years later, when I served as editor of the *Virginia Quarterly Review*, I encountered a letter in the journal's archive written by my predecessor Lambert Davis to H. L. Mencken seeking a contribution to the pages of the *VQR*. Davis suggested several topics to the famed "Sage of Baltimore," but Mencken settled on writing an essay on the difficulties facing the modern South, which also issued a stinging critique of the Agrarians. In "The South Astir," published in January 1935, Mencken argued that the South "may never sit down in formal and plenary session, as the Agrarians and Regionalists appear to sit down." Instead, a change to the idea of Southern identity was necessary, Mencken argued, for outdated ideas to be "forced gradually into the backwaters of the Southern domain."

How I wished I had read Mencken's words several decades earlier. Perhaps they would have helped me see that I did not have to distance myself from the South as I moved into adulthood.

The writers whose words fill the pages of this broad and diverse collection remind me of our region's seemingly constant quest to define itself. These poems captured my attention because they redefine poetry about the South as well as what we categorize as Southern poetry. Southern poetry can't be placed in a tidy box, since it is as varied as the writers themselves. There are many Souths, and many of those Souths are represented in the carefully crafted words of the poets encountered in this collection. Food is a common thread connecting these poems, and it's not just grits, greens, and pork—though they are here—but there's also menudo and matzoh balls, since these foods are also part of life and tradition in the South. As the late Jake Adam York wrote in his poem "Grace," "meals are memorials" and

> history moves in us as we raise
> our voices and then our glasses
> to pour a little out for those
> who poured out everything for us,
> we pour ourselves for them,
> so they can eat again.

York's poem is a fitting final poem in this collection, since it speaks to the idea of Southern identity, which rests at the heart of this collection. Each poet approaches the concept of what one might call Southernness with a great deal of versatility. In that search for identity and its connection with the past these poems reflect a growing and evolving South, one at odds with the old Agrarian idea of one tightly and strictly defined South. Instead these poets speak with voices that embrace many Souths.

The Agrarian ideal may have been constructed on a moonlight and magnolias fantasy of the South, a misguided attempt to freeze the region in time. This collection reveals why John Crowe Ransom, Allen Tate, and to a lesser extent, Robert Penn Warren had nothing to fear of changes coming to the region in the post–World War II era. In fact, the South these poets describe would be recognizable to the Agrarians since the historic South is connected with the contemporary—and ever changing—idea of the South. Honorée Fanonne Jeffers evokes the rural South in "The Gospel of Barbecue" when she writes "December is the best / time for hog killing." Naomi Shihab Nye captures the constancy of summer in the region when she describes it as "motion going out and memory coming in" in "Going for Peaches, Fredericksburg, Texas." A chain of memory connects these poems, one that reveals a shared connection as well as broader circle of what it means to be Southern.

The South is still a region of its own, but it is changing and evolving from the land that the Agrarians once knew, and that change is a source of its strength. It is a region filled with continuity in its sense of place as well as discontinuity in the ways that its sense of place is being transformed. The poems in *Vinegar and Char* reveal the ways the South may be morphing into something new but also provide windows into spaces where we can take refuge in its deep and complicated past. It is that complex, surprising, and unpredictable and ever changing South in which I take my stand. This collection reminds me that I am not alone and that there are others who are taking the very same stand in the very same idea of a broader and more inclusive South.

—W. RALPH EUBANKS

Vinegar & Char

We have memorized America,
how it was born and who we have been and where.
In ceremonies and silence we say the words,
telling the stories, singing the old songs.
We like the places they take us. Mostly we do.
The great and all the anonymous dead are there.
We know the sound of all the sounds we brought.
The rich taste of it is on our tongues.
But where are we going to be, and why, and who?

> —MILLER WILLIAMS,
> from "Of History and Hope"

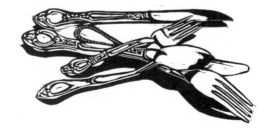

Lard Poetica   *An Introduction*

For more than three decades, my mother has served black-eyed peas for breakfast on New Year's Day. Some years this means a pot warm on the stove; some years, a container handed off the day before; once, packed into her flight carry-on luggage. She began doing this as a nod to my father's parents, both born and raised in Texas. My grandmother Peggy wasn't much of a cook—in fact, my father has a lifelong aversion to tomatoes, spinach, olives, and anything else she pried out of a can to feed four children. But Peggy had certain traditions. The pitcher of Bloody Marys on Christmas morning took some getting used to for my mother, but the black-eyed peas came easy.

Now, on the rare occasion the family is all in one place, my mother cooks two batches of black-eyed peas. Some simmer with ham hock and some with broth, since my sister is vegetarian. My sister cuts a square of cornbread, which I avoid since I'm allergic to milk and eggs. I make a Bloody Mary for my mother and myself, which my father regards as a traitorous invasion of tomato. We come together, and we toast the year ahead.

Traditions can be celebrated without being overly simplified. The Southern Foodways Alliance invites all who gather at the table to consider the history and the future of the American South in a spirit of respect and reconciliation. We tell our stories of changing traditions through the foods we eat, and many of the SFA's remarkable contributions to documenting culture occur at the margins of what was previously championed as iconic Southern cuisine. Benne seed seasons a Gullah dish. We travel the Delta's Tamale Trail. Serve up the slugburgers. Add sun-dried rabbit to our larder.

To assemble *Vinegar and Char*, we began with poets who have shared their work at SFA symposia or on the pages of SFA's *Gravy* quarterly. As editor, I was fortunate in the quality and breadth of connections already at hand. They comprised about half of the contributors; the rest was up to me. We took only one poem per poet, to ensure space for many voices. I sought emerging and established poets with connections to a geographic stretch spanning

Mississippi, Alabama, Florida, Georgia, South Carolina, North Carolina, Virginia, Kentucky, Tennessee, Arkansas, Texas, and Louisiana. We include voices from the Appalachian parts of West Virginia and Ohio. We feature those who immigrated with Cuban family to Miami. Sitting down to order the table of contents, I felt like a quilt maker trusted with fabric of every imaginable pattern and hue.

In the first section, we map lands inflected both by honest harvest and industries built on each other's backs. We confront killing what we wish to consume—animal, vegetable, or legume.

> . . . Wounded
> God of the Ground, Our Lady
> of Perpetual Toil & Dark Luck,
> harbor me & I pledge each
> inch of my waist not to waste
> you,

promises Kevin Young's "Prayer for Black-Eyed Peas." The second section examines modes of engagement fostered by food: friendship, lust, justice, commerce. "My father was a restaurant," recalls the speaker of "such as," a poem by Wo Chan: "Every noon he fed his lungs to an entire city." The third section recognizes how a meal provides for connection and communion, whether sincere or ironic.

> . . . [A]round here they'll give you something
> with olives and ham and Swiss on a
> goddamn garlic focaccia,

swears the speaker in "Eating a Muffaletta in Des Moines," by Brian Spears, before offering a corrective—"Come by my house. I'll make the bread."

We have focused on living poets, with the exception of Jake Adam York (1972–2012), whose poem lends our title phrase, "Vinegar and Char." I reached out to Jake the first time I came to Oxford, to serve as the University of Mississippi Summer Poet in Residence, since I'd be staying in a house that he'd occupied the year before. He advised two things: Watch out for bees in the mailbox, and if possible host a whole-hog roast in the backyard. He was not joking about either one. York and Miller Williams, the acclaimed Arkansas poet quoted in this collection's epigraph, believed in poetry's ability to create community, interrogate history, and delight the ear.

These poems are accompanied by custom works on paper, rich with chiaroscuro, by artist Julie Sola. Sola was a designer for six years with the famed Hatch Show Print in Nashville, Tennessee; her larger body of work celebrates music, animals, folklores, and motifs drawn from her Mexican heritage. Here, she took inspiration from our contributors. Sola transfers original drawings to linoleum, which she then carves. After the ink is applied, she rubs the paper with a wooden spoon before pulling the image away by hand.

Often, an introduction places the book within a larger canon. The older I get, the more I grow weary of canonical impulses, whether ranking authors or varieties of hot sauce. So let me advocate for a different kind of positioning. Please don't keep this book on a high shelf, waiting for the day when you can read it in full. Instead, stash it in your kitchen. Browse for the number of minutes it takes the crabs to boil, or peppers to blister, or grits to thicken. Graze three poems at a time, or reread the same poem three times. Smudge these pages with hoisin sauce. Please devour these verses.

With this volume, we mark two decades of Southern Foodways Alliance work, with more to come. In his 1999 letter recruiting SFA's founding forces, the late John Egerton offered his hope that we might "sit down and break bread together." The talented staff is tireless in pursuing that vision, with the support of the Center for the Study of Southern Culture at the University of Mississippi. I thank, in particular, John T. Edge and Sara Camp Milam. John T. had faith I could handle this anthology; Sara Camp made sure I did, step by step. Thanks also to my husband, Champneys Taylor, who has fielded many a late-night or early-morning conversation about this project.

"Over the years since I left home," Edna Lewis wrote, "I have kept thinking about the people I grew up with and about our way of life. I realize how much the bond that held us had to do with food." A signature quality of SFA events is that meals are not a practical afterthought, or a mere consequence of coming together. Each repast is a collaborative centerpiece, an opportunity for making new bonds. These poems are a virtual enactment of that phenomenon: collective light fed through the prism, refracted into many individual and remembered traditions. A family is forged on these pages.

—SANDRA BEASLEY

Section I

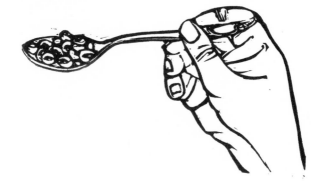

Times Like These: Marianna, Florida

One woe is past; &, behold, there come two woes more hereafter.
        —Revelation 9:12

In one field, husks, muscadine vines & a sugarcane graveyard furrow acres aching for the devil to beat his wife. In another, a skein of maggots & mayflies, musk thick & resolute, jockey for the cow's afterbirth. Down Old U.S. Road, weevils wheeze & chafed bales of hay settle for the wind's sneezes. *Wait for a sign,* the couple says & set their table with damask, fresh-pressed for a feast of sardines & cornbread. Train their child in the way he should babble. From dusk till dusk, they lull the boy with tales of a faraway sea, buckets of oysters to shuck. *OurFatherwhichartinheavenhallowedbethynamethykingdomcome thywillbedoneonearthasitisinheaven.* Still no rain. From dusk till dusk, they till dust. They reach for locks of hair & black-eyed peas, stowed away for times like these.

        —L. Lamar Wilson

Cook

kitchen
out back

a
way from buckra
who saunter
where he please
inside up and down
me

a
way from his wife
who scratch out fancy menus
seasoned with my tongue
hand
and tenderness

the only real pleasure
be my babies,
a small patch of something
where I grow okra and tomatoes,
and the name I will give myself
when I'm free
Mariah
Cook(e)

—KELLY NORMAN ELLIS

Vocabulary Lesson

Cornbread, cracklin' bread, bannock,
skillet cake, ash cake, hoe cake,

journey cake, Johnny cake, corn pone,
or *pane* or *poon* or *apoon* or *ponap,*

Indian pudding, hasty pudding, hush puppy,
grits—some words for what can be made

of cornmeal, simplest food a person
can grow and grind herself.

The vernacular so varied, it seems
uncommon. The uncommon so numerous,

it sounds of abundance.
391 phrases for cornbread

have been recorded. Beyond that count,
there's how whole kernel is used:

Hominy, big hominy, rockahominy,
hoppin' John, limpin' Susan, succotash,

creamed, cut, on the cob.
As seed in the Southern soil.

In the place I began, one thing
has put up such silk-tasseled possibilities.

How have I so often said *hungry*?
When the ways of being fed are so many?

—ROSE MCLARNEY

Shucking

My father lets down
The little drawbridge of his pickup truck,
A span of plywood planks on the back gate
Held level by hook and chain,
And dumps from the damp burlap
A load of locked doors
We've bought to break and enter,
Taking our spade-shaped knives
To the sharp and silted ridges of the oyster shells.

Almost safe inside the heavy canvas gloves,
Mule-brand, the fingers chewed through
By snags of ragged metal his acetylene
Cut back from the junked bodies of cars,
We look for leeways in the trap,
Any edge the blade can pry and widen,
Leverage to spring the hinge. I set aside
The hard ones for my father's savvy hands.
From the lusters of the bottom lid,
We split the raw attachments
And pour it all in a plastic pail—
Brine and gill plates and mantle—
My mother's turn now to turn
This plump meat seasoned by the sea
Into soups and stews and po-boy loaves
(Dredged in cornmeal, drowned in deep fat).

It's one more long Sunday when dinner waits
For my brother to drive down, late,
Through the pinesap airs of Hammond,
And for my sister to bring herself, late,
Across the white bridges, twin humps
On the billowed back of Lake Pontchartrain.

And so my father and I stand opening
The closed chambers, the cold valves,
And from these cups of calcium
Drink to each other a liquid
Of salt and grit, the oysters
Easing down like lumps in the throat.

—ELTON GLASER

Family Style

Papaw baked a big biscuit
in a cast iron skillet each morning.

Papa Dave took his breakfast
at the Court Café.

Jo made cornbread with less salt
than soda.

Ruby considered meat loaf poor-do.

Papaw liked to saucer
thick black coffee.

Papa Dave couldn't stand
to see mixed-up food.

Jo drank syrup.

Ruby took the skin off a chicken
neat as a coat off a child.

Papaw loved clabber.

Papa Dave relished canned peaches
with saltines.

Jo made a pan of icing,
then ate it.

Ruby left her chickens to air dry.

Papaw expected three pies
every Saturday lunch.

Papa Dave's sawmill cook
kept Ruby in berries.

Jo beat the devil out of steak
with a saucer edge.

The devil was tough
at Ruby's house too.

Papaw once for a year
drank beer before breakfast.

Papa Dave for his ulcers ate
cakes of yeast.

At Thanksgiving's feast, Jo
served tomato and kraut juice.

Ruby's remedy was milk toast,
domestic tea.

Papaw brought hamburgers
from the bus station Sunday evenings.

Papa Dave drove us in the Nash
for a cone of cream.

Jo's recipe for corn:
Boil the water while you go to the field.

Ruby's jam cake still
sweetens my days.

—GEORGE ELLA LYON

Carlo Flunks the Seventh Grade

Come a toad-strangler that day, I remember.
Kids wobble off the bus, umbrellas blooming.
Three bullies, white American, thowed rocks
at Splendi Pretti's creamy little leg.
I watch, too frayed to fight. Oh how she holler,
lord, run and dance, holding her head! Three big girl,
white American too, make them boy stop.

Same day, Miss Snodgrass take Splendi's sack lunch,
homemade garlic bread and *lonza*, set it
on the sill outside the window. Did the same
to Antonio's and Dominic's, and let
the white Americans hee-haw monstrous loud,
"Tommy Salami and Tony Baloney!
Tommy Salami and Tony Baloney!"
She pass my desk and say, "Charlie, I need
to put your lunch out, too. It has an odor."

I fire back, "Must be your lunch, Miss Snotgrass.
Mine's a poke sallet sandwich, ribbon cane,
and hickory nuts."

She say, "Show it to me."

I grab my sack and say, "You want to see,
I let you see all right." I tump it out
on my desk, grip the hickory nut hammer,
say, "You know, Miss Snotgrass, this girl here
goes home a-hungry nearbout every day
'cause a stray dog paw through her sack and gobble
all her good food."

I stand. Teacher snap, "Carlo!
You sit your little bottom down this second!"

But something ail me like I done gone deef
and seeing through a hazy blur a smoke.
My body burning cold, like snow-bit hands
when you run hot water over them. "No need
to fool with pushing up that window," say I,
and swing my hickory hammer through the glass.
Crack like thin ice. I flunk the seventh grade
over that stunt and mighty proud I did.

— GREG BROWNDERVILLE

How to Kill a Hog

Do you remember how close
you were to her

when she was farrowing
and she needed you

her bawling drawing
you out of bed

a bad dream
how you washed her vulva, soft

warm water over your own
hands how you scrubbed

even your fingernails
under your fingernails

before you came to the pen
and the sunflower oil you coated yourself in

so she would not chafe
even as she hemorrhaged

and how against all this
bloody shit and hay

you took each piglet
out of her night and into yours

into your palm and cleared
its mouth its nose of mucus

how you brought breath
to each set of tiny lungs

how you washed
how you opened her?

That is how to touch her now

Once she is hung
and cut straight cut

from rectum to neck
while the other men

take their cigarettes
find quick coffee, food

Lag behind wait
until the barn is empty

until you are alone
Then step inside her

your arms inside her
death like it is a room

your private room
peculiar and clean

Gather her organs up
into your arms

like you once did your mother's robes
when you were a boy who knew nothing

but the scent of sweat and silk
Hold her and inhale

Before reaching all the way around
to snip the last tendon

before you cut the stomach
intestines kidney liver

before you cut her heart
out

and she drops into you
and drops down

into the cold wash tub
of this day

close your eyes just once
just once

do not turn away

—Rebecca Gayle Howell

Boy

Boy, let me have a taste of that Mister Misty.
No, they brought it out around the time you
were born in sixty. I like the way it swish
in the cup. Sound like Sammy Davis Jr.
doing the soft shoe shuffle. They call
that the sand dance. Sound like shifting grains
or a fast train. Them little bits of ice
tap your teeth, and you can chew on that sweet
mouthful of cold melting to nothing before
you swallow it down. First time I had one
of these, I drank it too fast, crystals in syrup
dancing around and down my throat chilled
like Christmas and New Year's cold breath moving
down to my chest. And if that wasn't enough,
then I felt like my head was about to split
right open. Thought my forehead was gon look
like that Dairy Queen sign red and wide
like a gash. You know, they ice cream got nothing
on your mama's pineapple ice cream. Theirs
ain't nothing but soft light ice milk. They build
it high like a steeple, but ain't nothing
to that either. You see your mama puts
a dozen eggs in her custard to make
it rich. The sound of the ice and salt shifting
in that bucket as it melts with that electric
churn's whining motor groaning as that ice
cream stiffens up sure is pleasing cause I know
the ice cream about ready. You know, there are
folks getting they heads split so we don't have
to go around to that side window no more.

— SEAN HILL

The Sacred and the Bread

The devil's mistake was telling Jesus
to make his own bread from stones.
He might have won the argument if
he'd taken the Son of Man to a kitchen
bathed in sunlight at the bottom
of a mountain where a creek with water
colder than January flows all year long.

There's an oven there and a bin with flour.
A white-haired woman knows her way
around the wooden table where she kneads,
shapes, molds loaves of pure love.

This is bread worth breaking.

In a little white church on top of a hill
we'd take communion and then take turns
carrying that ragged loaf home for dinner.
　　　　Bread too sacred to scatter.
Instead we'd butter slices and sink our teeth
into softness handcrafted like quilts.
This was bread stitched with love, faith,
and a peace that, like yeast, raised us all.

The Word is made manifest in crumb and crust.
This is a truer translation, and the devil . . . well,
maybe he can't recognize real temptation.
The truth is so often hidden in plain sight.

Yes, the devil tried the wrong seduction.
Man does not live by bread alone.
What that old serpent really needed
was a spoon and a jar of apple butter.

—SARAH LOUDIN THOMAS

Saltine

How well its square
fit my palm, my mouth,
a toasty wafer slipped
onto the sick tongue
or into chicken soup,

each crisp saltine a tile
pierced with 13 holes
in rows of 3 and 2,
its edges perforated
like a postage stamp,

one of a shifting stack
sealed in wax paper
whose noisy opening
always signaled *snack*,
peanut butter or cheese

thick inside Premiums,
the closest we ever got
to serving *hors d'oeuvres*:
the redneck's hardtack,
the cracker's cracker.

—Michael McFee

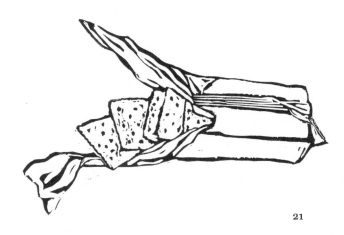

Fanny Says How to Make Potato Salad

Alright now. What you got to do is get some potatoes, I used to buy them big bags of Idaho potatoes, and you need to wursh them real good and boil them whole. Now, you know how your mama cooks, like this—*plom, plom, plom*—so just drop those fuckers in the water and don't worry about them till they get soft enough to just peel with your thumbs, but not too soft, cause we're making salad here, not mashed potatoes.

So then you've got to get you one stalk a celery, the whole thing now, and peel back them big strings, cause nobody wants to have to pick their teeth while they trying to smile at you telling you your salad's any good. And chop up that celery, and then you do the same to one green pepper, not the green onion, now, but the pepper, round-like and overpriced in the grocery store.

Boil and chop you four eggs. Also need you about six a them sweet pickles I love so much at Thanksgiving on the Lazy Susan. You can chop them up, or if you want, you can use a bit of that canned pickle relish your uncle always slopped on them nasty-ass hot dogs of his.

Also add one onion, chopped, and try to use a white one, especially them good old Vidalia onions, they not nearly as strong as the yella. Besides, you don't want to blow nobody out with your breath.

You need one a them big bowls, you know, about this big around, and mix it all real good with your hands. Now you know you got to have a little salt and pepper, and three tablespoons or so a mayonnaise, or if you want to make it the real way I used to like, use Miracle Whip. Now, be careful now with that mayo, make sure that shit's fresh or you'll ruin the whole batch and have everybody in the house running to the bathroom. Also add in about the same amount a plain yella mustard. You know, the kind that's yella as a gourd and comes in one a them round bottles.

While you're mixing it with your hands, bring the bottom to the top. You might even want to add a jar a pimentos for color. Now, be sure and take a bite in your mouth before you serve it—it's gotta have a little wang in it, it can't be dull. If it is, add a little bit a sugar or vinegar to it.

Cover it up and let it sit in the fridge for one hour. It should be enough to last you three or four nights, and of course, if your husband's coming home, you might want to make it all pretty by putting it all on top a some lettuce leaves and dusting it with a little a that paprika.

—NICKOLE BROWN

Livers and Gizzards

Water the secret to these offal
simple recipes, the wet dark blood
soaking the spongy organ no weight
of pungent flavor could hold against
the splatter of angry grease flying
from the roiling clouds of the fryer
like arcing bolts of sear and burn
fusing heat's tattoo script on skin.
But the muscle of grist softens
in the pressure of steam's boil
until the whistle valve spits forth
the stinging mist of essence's stink,
the knot of chew readying its rubber
gravel pop for the willing mouth
through a slow crusted sink and
rise in the surface of the gold bath.
Both wait and wait for that special
tongue, mother wit hungry for half-
or full pints of one, the other, or
sometimes both, transitory crispy
nuggets sweating and drying out
until gut goes to gut or trash, when
what is thrown away is prized or lost.

—JON TRIBBLE

My Stove's in Good Condition

Because she thought I wanted it,

    for dinner Naomi wants catfish,
      catfish on the range spitting oil, its smoke
        spicing the house with pepper, black & cayenne.

From speakers in the living room, ragtime piano,

    a winking old blues by Lil Johnson,
      Lil Johnson singing about her stove but fooling
        with more than pots & pans: *When my wood gets too hot* . . .

I check the crisp on the fish & flip, then shuffle in my slippers

    to the front windows, looking for Naomi to pull up at the house,
      brick house down the street from the Poplar Bridge,
        built in '22 & crumbling over the freight rail line.

No sign of her little blue car,

    just the 32 bus ferrying riders from North Philly,
      North Philly to graveyard shifts downtown,
        guards & clerks & cleaners in the lit cabin

like relatives waiting in a hospice room:

    a man presses his forehead against a window,
      window pushing up the brim of his cap: a gray woman
        slouches down & pillows her head on plastic bags stuffed

with plastic bags & piled on the next seat. Watching for Naomi,

    I'd lost the fish & music, then again the crackling,
      crackling of cornmeal & pepper, of Lil Johnson
        & her lusty blues: *Nothin to be waitin on, let's get drunk*

and truck. A month since we lay curled & sweaty in bed:

on the way back to the kitchen, I turn down the music,
   music that growled like hunger, growled like the dull ache
   of hunger filling the body, pushing out till the mind

pricks with hunger, is consumed with hunger—

so much hunger in these blues:
                              blues so much hunger:
         hunger so much blues:
                                             so much blues:
               hunger:
                                    hunger:
so much:
                           blues:
         hunger so much:
                     blues:
         so much:
                           blues:
         hunger:
                     blues

   —IAIN HALEY POLLOCK

Singing to Make Butter Come

To coax the butter to appear, you raise
the plunger, drive it in the crock, and drive
it down again. But sometimes if it's hot
or if the air's too moist or pressure low,
no matter how you stir and dash and beat,
the clabber yields no butter. Sour milk stays
sour milk. You shake and beg the blinky swill,
and nothing makes the butter come. You feel
there's evil in the air, a curse is on
the chemistry and on your labor. Then's
the time to calm yourself and stay yourself
and whisper to the crock of clabber, sing
a slow, sad ballad or a hymn to soothe
the troubled sour. And soon the bits appear
like flakes of snow out of the depths, and more
rise like the dead at Resurrection, join
their tips and soaring bodies in the light
to form, from the corruption's thickening,
a sweet and firm and perfect gathering.

—ROBERT MORGAN

Sugar Cane at the A&P

Purple as it used to be in the field,
a few stalks, trimmed, stand gaunt
in the corner among fruit piles, bins
of seed, story poles taking measure.
Priced like cooking greens or kale
so much a stalk, they'll go to a right
buyer, sudden emblems of early
poaching years ago from neighboring
farms, breaking off sections to peel
with a short pocket knife, chewing
the pulp, sweet juice new as candy.
Spitting out chaff, we made our own
piles of bagasse, trying hard to hide
any sound, protected by the covering
leaves we thought safe, ears to wind,
ready to run if anyone came looking.
Years later purple rises from a field
to stand in a store, revenant,
like cotton planted half a block off
the river in somebody's front yard
or on the Earhart neutral ground
collecting oil dust from passing cars,
pitched echoes measuring memory.
Two days later, the cane was gone
and never found, there or anyplace,
the store wall's blank white pages
staring at me with nothing left to say.

—GARLAND STROTHER

Drill

Mama talks in this one.

Here's us, backing down our driveway's maze of red-dirt dog-legs, her at the wheel (with a fresh-forged license), me turned around navigating, the yard black-dark but flushed now (and now) and now with brake-lights, her Kool-tip flaring on every hard in-breath, river-reek and oil-scorch and marsh-gas mingling, our under-chassis (and rear axle, eyeteeth) chuttering due to roots and rain-ruts, our rust-crusting Rambler swerving and fishtailing and near-missing trees.

At the mailbox, gears knock, gnaw, grind, find Forward eventually: we're missile-heading straight (more or less) for the LowCountry fairgrounds; here's us, late, loud, breaknecking her blue-ribbon hoard to the Fair.

Everything is home-made.

Not just our back-seat freight of gem-flame jelly-jars (slip-skin grape, beet, black- and blueberry, brunt-apple, seed-splacked fig) and payload of pressure-torqued pickle-jars (wrick-kinked banana-peppers, lethal hot-hat peppers, (green) tear-tomatoes, hairy okra, baby-dills in brine), but also the crazy quilt safe-swaddling them, the gummed saliva-labels neat-naming them, my mama's name —hieroglyphical, grease-penciled, *'KAY' (KAZUE) HUTTO*— branding lids.

Do you reckon tomorrow they'll put my picture in the paper?

Will somebody do a write-up when I win?

—ATSURO RILEY

When My Mother Is Away

My father, who hasn't cooked since they were married,
since he came up to the mountains from the coast,
makes red beans sweating with andouille,
leaves them all day to soak, then simmer on the stove.

When I call, he is too busy for the telephone.
The baseball game is on, the rice is on,
and if he lets it cook too long it goes to glue.
You know, sweetheart, he says, *I have to pay attention to the stove.*

My father goes home when our house is empty.
The days he spends alone: that false blank pulse
of the hurricane's eye on his boyhood city. Inside
his mother bends and dices celery beside the stove

and cooks it to invisible. You have to take it slow
and gentle if you want to get it right, and boil
the beans low to keep the skin from breaking.
She had patience for the heat and for the stove

and nothing else. This one accumulation she could take.
My father likes the whole mess peppered strong, one bite
enough to manufacture weather on his face: the moment
when he brings it to his mouth, the moment the storm breaks.

—MOLLY MCCULLY BROWN

Prayer for Black-Eyed Peas

Humbly, I come to you now
O bruised lord, beautiful
wounded legume,
in this time of plague, in my
very need. Ugly angel,
for years I have forsaken
you come New Year's Day,
have meant to meet you
where you live & not
managed to. I gave you up
like an unfaithful lover, but still
you nag me like a mother.
Like the brother I don't have
I need you now to confide in,
my eyes & yours darkened
by worry, my baby
shoes bronzed & lost.
Awkward antidote,
bring me luck & whatever
else you choose & I'll bend low
to shore you up. Part
of me misses you, part knows
you'll never leave, the rest
wants you to hear my every
unproud prayer. Wounded
God of the Ground, Our Lady
of Perpetual Toil & Dark Luck,
harbor me & I pledge each
inch of my waist not to waste
you, to clean my plate
each January & like you
not look back. You are
like the rice & gravy my Great
Aunt Toota cooked—you need,
& I with you, nothing else.

Holy sister, you are my father
planted along the road
one mile from where he
was born, brought full
circle, almost. You, the visitation
I pray for & what vision
I got—not quite
my father's second sight.
My grandmother saying
she dreams of me
& he every night. *Every*
night. Every night.
Small book of hours, quiet
captain, you are our future
born blind, eyes swole shut,
or sewn.

—KEVIN YOUNG

Section II

Mango, Number 61

Pescado grande was number 14, while *pescado chico*, was number 12; *dinero*, money, was number 10. This was *la charada*, the sacred and obsessive numerology my *abuela* used to predict lottery numbers or winning trifectas at the dog track. The grocery stores and pawn shops on Flagler Street handed out complimentary wallet-size cards printed with the entire *charada*, numbers 1 through 100: number 70 was *coco*, number 89 was *melón* and number 61 was *mango*. Mango was Mrs. Pike, the last *americana* on the block with the best mango tree in the neighborhood. *Mamá* would coerce her in granting us picking rights—after all, *los americanos don't eat mango*, she'd reason. Mango was fruit wrapped in brown paper bags, hidden like ripening secrets in the kitchen oven. Mango was the perfect house warming gift and a marmalade dessert with thick slices of cream cheese at birthday dinners and Thanksgiving. Mangos, watching like amber cat's eyes. Mangos, perfectly still in their speckled maroon shells like giant unhatched eggs. Number 48 was *cucaracha*, number 36 was *bodega*, but mango was my uncle's bodega, where everyone spoke only loud Spanish, the precious gold fruit towering in *tres-por-un-peso* pyramids. Mango was mango shakes made with milk, sugar and a pinch of salt—my grandfather's treat at the 8th street market after baseball practice. Number 60 was *sol*, number 18 was *palma*, but mango was my father and I under the largest shade tree at the edges of Tamiami Park. Mango was *abuela* and I hunched over the counter covered with the Spanish newspaper, devouring the dissected flesh of the fruit slithering like molten gold through our fingers, the nectar cascading from our binging chins, *abuela* consumed in her rapture and convinced that I absolutely loved mangos. Those messy mangos. Number 79 was *cubano*—us, and number 93 was *revolución*, though I always thought it should be 58, the actual year of the revolution—the reason why, I'm told, we live so obsessively and nostalgically eating number 61s, *mangos*, here in number 87, *América*.

—Richard Blanco

Curry

I bring each one to you after I grind it,
still in the mortar, warm and pungent you
lie there on the sofa watching me; I look
at you as I grind each spice,
feel your eyes stippling the back of my legs
and neck. I turn to your eyes again and again:
they know what I can do with these spices—
garlic and ginger, turmeric and abundant
red pepper—I grind them together, mix them
into yogurt white as my camisole,
rub the chicken pieces with the spiced yogurt,
yellow from the turmeric and red pepper.
I pierce the skin with a fork, leave the kitchen
to go to you in the next room, to rub
my hands of spiced yogurt and raw chicken
on your chest and thighs. I want to pierce you,
I want my hands to be full of you, of your eyes
pretending a rope is wrapped around arms and legs,
pretending all you can do is look at me
in just this camisole, and the fresh-ground pepper—

Our voices whisper what we will do
when we finish; our voices are cumin
and coriander, mustard seed and nutmeg,
cilantro, saffron and cinnamon;
just-crushed cardamom and allspice, almonds
and onions, shredded coconut, butter and cloves,
lemon, and your eyes that meet mine as I take off
the camisole, and the rubbed chicken and Marsala
begin to heat up, all the spices mingling,
pepper-rich, blood-thick.

—SHERYL ST. GERMAIN

Backbone

Nana would say, *Come here child. What kind of comb does you mother use?* And then I would sit between her legs, where the bluish, flowery dressing gown spread over the reddish, flowery wingback. Howl as she dragged that paddle brush through my naps and rounds. *Hush girl.* I would grimace and spit and let tears itch up the corners of my eyes, staying still though, as she smoothed my scalp with the sweat off her highball—Glenlivet, 11:00 am, every day, come breast or bone, brain or lung—and wove the tufts into a fluffy braid half down my back. *Cancer? Hell.*

She'd turn on the Vivaldi, pat her chemo bag, teach me Spades. Aunt Wendy curled her hair for late church, and Daddy looked on, long faced, at us all. I would reach for a card and, *Ashy. Turn around and let me get some of this on you.* The Vaseline was always in a jar next to the lamp, behind the whiskey and the remote control. *It looks like you've been crawling around in flour on your knees and elbows.* Nana made those joint bones glisten, she did,

died, and my cousin, out loud
she wrote a menu, said—
I know how to make cheesecake,
I know how to make shrimp,
I can fix corn pone, potatoes.

But me, I knew in secret
how to make a shiny elbow
out of flour and Vaseline,
how to make a rope hang
from my head
with screams and scotch sweat.

—Caroline Randall Williams

Like Father

My father's embrace is tighter
Now that he knows
He is not the only man in my life.
He whispers, *Remember when*, and, *I love you*,
As he holds my hand hungry
For a discussion of Bible scriptures
Over breakfast. He pours cups of coffee
I can't stop
Spilling.

My father's embrace is firm and warm
Now that he knows. He begs forgiveness
For anything he may have done to make me
Turn to abomination
As he watches my eggs, scrambled
Soft. Yolk runs all over the plate.
A rubber band binds the morning paper.

My father's embrace tightens. Grits
Stiffen. I hug back
Like a little boy, gripping
To prove his handshake.
Daddy squeezes me close,
But I cannot feel his heartbeat
And he cannot hear mine—
There is too much flesh between us,
Two men in love.

—JERICHO BROWN

Canning Memories

Indian summer Saturday mornings
meant project door screens sat open
waiting for the vegetable truck

No new moons or first frosts,
just the horn on an old flatbed
trumpeting the harvest

No almanac announcement, no ads
just a short black farmer in overalls
and mud-caked boots

Grandmothers who still clicked
their tongues, who called up the sound
of a tractor at daybreak,
the perfume of fresh turned earth
and the secret location of the best
blackberry patch
like they were remembering
old lovers, planted themselves
a squint away from palming
and weighing potatoes
string beans, kale, turnips, sweet corn
onions and cabbage

They seeded themselves
close enough to see each other
bent low in the fields, pulling weeds

dispensing verbal insecticide
gingham dresses gathered in front
cradling cucumbers and Big Boy tomatoes
destined for kitchen window sills
and mason jars

They break sacred ground far away
from these acres of red brick
and concrete neighbors
to be close enough to the earth
to know
  if all city folk plant iz family 'n friends
  alls dey gonna gets iz funerals

—FRANK X WALKER

Food Stamps

Ma'am,
I am standing directly on the yellow line,
the line looks backward and ahead.
Cars drive through me because I am thinking
right here in the middle of Need Mo' Street,
listening to myself being crushed underfoot.

I will move,
I will scrape myself from the pavement
(when I am less busy).
I will walk to Gramma's in summertime
and curl my hair with hot comb heat.
I will chew bacca and dip snuff
because I always wanted caramel spit.
I will dance in my bag of secrets
because poetry is a thinking woman's job,
like welfare is poetry
and waiting in WIC lines is, too.

Ma'am,
poetry don't ask for a thinking woman's income
so why the hell do you?

—SHIRLETTE AMMONS

Talk Radio, D.C.

Leave fatback and a copper penny
on a wound 'til it draw out the poison,
'til the penny turn green.

Tobacco's what works on a bee-sting,
but for poison ivy—I'm serious, now—
catch your first morning urine in your hands
and splash it on that rash.

When they had the diptheria epidemic
I was burning up with fever, burning and burning.
When the doctor left the house, my grandmother
snuck in the back door with a croaker sack of mackerel.
The next morning, my fever had broke
and the fish was all cooked.

—ELIZABETH ALEXANDER

Ode

my Spanish is an itchy phantom limb;
it is reaching for words and only finding air.
 —Melissa Lozada-Oliva, "My Spanish"

We are disappointments—we cannot make good of grief by giving it back to the tortilla, like my grandmother, burning it off her fingertips & into the dough, the front burner, a novela in flames. We are unlit pilot light—she, Virginia Slim. We eat her smoke, we landscape the hot discs with butter that glistens & pearls like the way *rr* leaves her mouth. We melt cheddar cheese. We add bacon & eggs, beans soaked overnight like her stubbornness. She cooks the bacon only to save the grease for the beans. She cooks the beans, then cooks the beans. *Tortilla* isn't a word that sounds like it lives anywhere near loss, but its location is mano, brazo, two places that have left the map of her. She tells us this is the last time she'll make them for us—she doesn't think she'll make it through many more nights of walking on water. The rolling pin hits the counter in its urgency, & we can't put love back where it came from like she does.

—Iliana Rocha

Knowing

A child of Depression, her blue-veined hands
map a life drawn from hilly acres, hands that
suckered tobacco, weeded corn, dug potatoes, endured
loss of child and man, palms open to help neighbors, kin.
On her front porch, she leans forward in painted chair,
breaks the tip of a half-runner, tugs string
down its spine. The pile grows like green spaghetti.
"Did you know the Chinese stir-fry green beans?"
asks a niece, the one who went to Europe junior year.
"And the French cut them slantwise with a knife."
"I simmer beans with a little fatback,
cook them hours, steam up the windows,
bake cornbread hot and crusty in the skillet
Mama left me." Mae says, "That is what I know."

—Sylvia Woods

such as

peril
fever   collection of pages
heavy

a hard
macaroni   and a quick brick

road

caution

dandelion
damp floor   a cracked saucer
of horseradish
of children   and lost suburbs

school bus of nostalgia   the oxbone kingdom

a river   a yolk
a sac
that

certain type of happiness

sliver
of bright butter

ripe lemon   dry urine
porch light
invisible

dull gold
fried blonde
firefly

corona

monster eye

such as

what to do when someone sings
so sweetly an epithet

is singing so sweetly   beside you
your epithet smiling and joyous
this god bless american

name a celebration
so heavenward and wrong

it touches me
to learn again and again
that this is my body   my dear and only body
one lovely chink in the whole damn night.

SUCH AS

My mother was a fever. My father was a restaurant.
Every noon he fed his lungs to an entire city.
Every night he held my belly searching for a suburb.
I was the firefly that flared only once in my father's kingdom.
I learned to speak English like a quick brick road. I split
rocks in the backlot of my father's skull.
I picked dandelions from the underarms of him, my father.
I was the smell of ripe lemons in his oxbone nation. I was never
brave. But, he let me eat butter, held me like an egg. I was pure yolk,
and ate everything with my monster eye.
Oh. Did I mention my mother was the fever? That was my father, actually.
Still my father pressed against the doorframe.
My father was always the fever and always the restaurant.
My father whose splintered shoulders knew the words to one anthem only.

—Wo Chan

It Is Simple

He walks the driveway
back to the house the
mail something he will
look through at the
table it is quiet on this
side of Mobile the lands
divided subdivided it is
only now & then a plane
might fly nearby enough
to remind anyone of the
places they've been or
the people they've lost
but never mind what is
sad that will come now
is the scent of garlic on
fingers as he opens a
letter from Italy & finds
no note only pieces to a
puzzle the father shakes
from an envelope on
the stove *chicken adobo*
juices cooking into layers
of meat until it is all the
same color like coffee
without milk the way the
son has learned to drink
it in Florence where
times he has paused
along the Ponte Santa
Trinita the Arno clouded
after a storm & thought
of him on one side of
the puzzle a few letters
half of a word & on the
other laminated colors

to a painting the father
spends an afternoon
putting together at the
kitchen table again the
scent of garlic on each
piece & then it is done the
father turns the picture
of the bridge over &
finds a message his son
has written it is simple
a phrase in Tagalog the
language between them

—JON PINEDA

River Politics

I spit my smack,

Jim slugs his Jack,

Rob stews his lack,

Carey prepares his rack,

herons hunker on blowdowns,

deer wait on high moon for their rounds,

and the campfire

might as well be an empire

we all

watch dissolve

(in the slough, a carp roll, a splash)

into ash.

—ADAM VINES

The Glory Be-B-Q

Not much to a roadside barbeque:
A smoker & a grill, a lean-to
   W/ a picnic table.
The menu, if there is a menu,
    Is just a list of victuals
    Someone's nailed
       To a fencepost or a tree:

    Baby backs (½ rack or full),
Cob corn, cornbread, pulled
      Pork, collard greens,
Smoked okra, apple
       Cabbage slaw, baked beans,
       BBQ chicken, sweet tea,
         Peach cobbler;

       & yet—. "Hopler!
    Brisket & black-eyed peas,
    Co'-Cola!" A breeze
Bedevils dust across the lot. A gull
      Circles w/ a bone in its beak.
A man on a motorcycle,
Deckle packed in a saddle-

    Bag, squeals his hog street-
Ward & back down the hill.
The pit master stokes coals
W/ the tip of a stick & blue
    Smoke blooms. The air, all
Cloud & tallow, yellows the rising moon.
Hell of a view.

    —JAY HOPLER

Liberty Street Seafood

I stand in line. Behind me the hungry stretch & wiggle
out the door. Sterling cake bowls nestle in ice:

mullet   striped bass   whiskered cat   rock shrimp
steel porgies   blue crab   "No eel 'til Christmas"

mother mussels   flat-face flounder   sleeping snapper
whiting   one sea turtle   (lazy fisherman).

In his fishmonger-owner apron Randy is white, round
as a blowfish, conducting this orchestra of desire.

Members: the cut boys and the lined up, who come
every day and wait in between frozen ice and hot oil.

The cut boys are well suited in fish scale and high up
on risers above us. They sing out with their knives.

Stationed inside tiny cutting booths slashing this throat
and that. Fish tune.

Veritas: Those who are exquisite at beheading
always occupy a throne.

One has a giant Afro. Another's hair is finely braided
backward, like flattened rows of corn. The half-straight

ends of his thick black wool curl up his neck like one large
fin. The last one has shaved and greased his head for duty.

Old men who sit around, outside the front door, tease.
Early on they named him, *Dolphin*. He is playful, jumpy,

slick, far more endangered than the other two. All three
wear the heavy rubber smocks of men who use their

hands to kill (& feed). All three hold knives longer than their
johnsons. For now, they are safe. The wet wood engulfs

them from waist down. Cleaned fish: their handiwork
will soon be on display at ninety-six dinner tables, Southside.

We pass the time by lying:

How you do?
Fine.

Alabaster fish scales streak & dot their hair like Mardi
Gras keepsakes. Fish petals float into the wet air.

Black. Indian. Zulu. Sequined, smelly, bloody scales settle
across three sets of brown hands, arms, in muscle shirts.

Scales thick as white evening gloves. The cut boys turn
each fish over like one-eyed fabric dolls. One has his

Mama Helene's eyelashes. He is the jittery dolphin
on the loose. A hand-me-down Afro pick sits in No. 2's

back pocket. This one with a tail always on his neck
has a fist always on his comb, circa 1975, belonging

to his brother, thrown under the jail, up under in upstate
Connecticut. Cause: a bad fight about a *chica* gone jugular.

These cut boys, shine jewel & scale, stationed before a wall
of black & silver ways & means. Eastern Star daughters and

North Star slaves stare out at the hungry through their
notched eyes. They whisper and laugh, loving how we wait

on them. Three Black boys in hip hop haute couture, in suits
of bloody, rubber smocks, standing side by side, making

three dollars an hour, beheading and detailing fish.
Their long knives whacking pine all day. Fish eyes roll.

So Friday is made. The white man reaches
for the money, faces the hungry,

his back fully turned,
their knives just above his head.

   —NIKKY FINNEY

Tableau

At breakfast, the scent of lemons,
just-picked, yellowing on the sill.
At the table, a man and woman.

Between them, a still life:
shallow bowl, damask plums
in one square of morning light.

The woman sips tea
from a chipped blue cup, turning it,
avoiding the rough white edge.

The man, his thumb pushing deep
toward the pit, peels taut skin
clean from plum flesh.

The woman watches his hands,
the pale fruit darkening
wherever he's pushed too hard.

She is thinking *seed*, the hardness
she'll roll on her tongue,
a beginning. One by one,

the man fills the bowl with globes
that glisten. *Translucent*, he thinks.
The woman, now, her cup tilting

empty, sees, for the first time,
the hairline crack
that has begun to split the bowl in half.

—Natasha Trethewey

Savannah Crabs

Bluish and thirsty, packed tight as oranges,
they come from the coast in the iced trunk
of the blue Buick our aunt drives. She's sunk
in thoughts of dinner and not the tinges

of dread that will stain her African violets
as she tends a back pain. She does not think
of her mother, who'll die this fall under pink
bedclothes without a goodnight; the eyelets

of her gown will spell the Chinese words
for *loneliness, lovelessness, white birds.*

When our aunt and her passengers get to town,
my brother and I crouch by the crate,
poke slow ones with sticks. Two escape;
our parents chase them with tongs around

the garden, then dump all seventy-four
in the laundry-room sink. They scuttle and flip
like fat gymnasts; they amaze us kids.
We salt them, singing *When it rains it pours.*

They spit back curses: *You'll ache; you'll smother;*
you'll never be able to talk to each other.

My aunt has brought me a spiny, off-yellow
shell, big as my hand. It sits
on the dryer, where I forget about it
to watch the steamer, where waving hello

and goodbye, the first mute batch reddens
and stills. I think of my shell and go back.
Out of it, welt-ridden legs grasp
no sand. He's ugly, a hermit, threatening.

I peer in his house and read the prophecy:
You'll find joy, but you must leave the family.

—ADRIENNE SU

Going for Peaches, Fredericksburg, Texas

Those with experience look for a special kind.
Red Globe, the skin slips off like a fine silk camisole.
Boy breaks one open with his hands. Yes, it's good,
my old relatives say, but we'll look around.
They want me to stop at every peach stand
between Stonewall and Fredericksburg,
leave the air conditioner running,
jump out and ask the price.

Coming up here they talked about
the best ways to die. One favors a plane crash,
but not over a city. One wants to makes sure
her grass is watered when she goes.
Ladies, ladies! This peach is fine,
it blushes on both sides.
But they want to keep driving.

In Fredericksburg the houses are stone,
they remind me of wristwatches, glass polished,
years ticking by in each wall.
I don't like stone, says one. What if it fell?
I don't like Fredericksburg, says the other.
Too many Germans driving too slow.
She herself is German as Stuttgart.
The day presses forward, wearing complaints
like charms on its bony wrist.

Actually ladies (I can't resist),
I don't think you wanted peaches after all,
you just wanted a nip of scenery,
some hills to tuck behind your heads.
The buying starts immediately, from a scarfed woman who says
I gave up teachin' for peachin'.
She has us sign a guest book.

One aunt insists on re-loading into her own box,
so she can see the fruit on the bottom.
One rejects any slight bruise.
But Ma'am, the seller insists, nature isn't perfect.
Her hands are spotted, like a peach.

On the road, cars weave loose patterns between lanes.
We will float in flowery peach-smell
back to our separate kettles, our private tables and knives,
and line up the bounty,
deciding which ones go where.
A canned peach, says one aunt, lasts ten years.
She was 87 last week. But a frozen peach
tastes better on ice cream.
Everything we have learned so far,
the stages of ripening alive in our skins,
on a day that was real to us, that was summer,
motion going out and memory coming in.

—NAOMI SHIHAB NYE

Acceptance Speech

The radio's replaying last night's winners
and the gratitude of the glamorous,
everyone thanking everybody for making everything
so possible, until I want to shush
the faucet, dry my hands, join in right here
at the cluttered podium of the sink, and thank

my mother for teaching me the true meaning of okra,
my children for putting back the growl in hunger,
my husband, *primo uomo* of dinner, for not
begrudging me this starring role—

without all of them, I know this soup
would not be here tonight.

And let me just add that I could not
have made it without the marrow bone, that blood-
brother to the broth, and the tomatoes
who opened up their hearts, and the self-effacing limas,
the blonde sorority of corn, the cayenne
and oregano who dashed in
in the nick of time.

Special thanks, as always, to the salt—
you know who you are—and to the knife,
who revealed the ripe beneath the rind,
the clean truth underneath the dirty peel.

—I hope I've not forgotten anyone—
oh, yes, to the celery and the parsnip,
those bit players only there to swell the scene,
let me just say: sometimes I know exactly how you feel.

But not tonight, not when it's all
coming to something and the heat is on and
I'm basking in another round
of blue applause.

       —LYNN POWELL

Bounty

In the dewy morning the cucumbers
you twisted from prickly garden vines

will darken and crisp on your yellow
kitchen table, preserving a memory

of tendrils crawling through wormy soil
and the broad leaves that canopied

them in the heated day. They remember
stretching from melon flowers. They

remember the bees who sugared
the stigma. Their seeds will tell you a story

of sowing and reaping, a tale suspended
in jelly, recited in your salads, read

in the Benedictine spread on your bread,
and tasted in an emerald grace.

—MARIANNE WORTHINGTON

Section III

Salat Behind Al's Mediterranean and American Food

This evening, in Birmingham,
when I'm meeting a friend
for fried chicken
and poetry,
you prostrate before God
on a piece of cardboard box
in the back alley.
Beside you, there is a dumpster
whispering styrofoam
and onion skins.
The shells of dead cockroaches
bend and crackle
under your knees. Even they pray.
The backdoor of the restaurant
and the towering
University Parking Deck
shelter you in shadow.
Fifteen minutes from now,
you will bring me cheap fries
and fingers,
and when you ask me
if I'd like ketchup,
your accent heavy as oil,
it sounds like a proverb—
clean tomato,
sovereign God.

—ASHLEY M. JONES

Jubilee

Come down to the water. Bring your snare drum,
your hubcaps, the trash can lid. Bring every
joyful noise you've held at bay so long.
The fish have risen to the surface this early
morning: flounder, shrimp, and every blue crab
this side of Mobile. Bottom feeders? Please.
They shine like your Grandpa Les' Cadillac,
the one you rode in, slow so all the girls
could see. They called to you like katydids.
And the springs in that car sounded like tubas
as you moved up and down. Make a soulful sound
unto the leather and the wheel, praise the man
who had the good sense to build a front seat
like a bed, who knew you'd never buy a car
that big if you only meant to drive it.

—Gabrielle Calvocoressi

Why It's Delicious

Because my grandmother marched out to the end
of the yard, threw the white oval seeds on the ground
and walked away, and almost overnight the tangle
of vines wrapped itself around the clothesline pole,
the fence and screened in porch. Then small green
pumpkins sprouted and brightened in places so odd
we had to move them to give them room to grow
or to keep them from breaking through the screen.
And when they were large and heavy, Mima ambled
out, lifted the pumpkins and carried them in to carve
and cook the chunks for days in soups, with rice and
with lemon. Except for a handful, she toasted
the seeds and we ate *pepitas* with salt, cracking shells
with our teeth to reach the slim green meat inside.

Because Jeanne's mom planted and tended a garden
that grew peas we shucked on her new husband's
farmhouse porch at the foot of a Pennsylvania mountain,
and she steamed them and served them for dinner
with chicken and mashed potatoes. Because that
bicentennial summer Jeanne and I joined her mom,
she arranged a net over blueberry bushes under which,
clever birds, we snuck to steal the dark ripe beads.
Because Jeanne's mom took us to pick fat strawberries
we boiled and stirred into jam in huge pots all day,
slathered on thick slices of airy Amish bread, and carried
home in mason jars sealed with paraffin, souvenirs.

Because the fleshy grapefruit in the neighbor's yard
overhanging our fence personally announces the coming
of winter in our central Florida town and is sweeter
and juicier than store-bought fruit I would never pay for,
and reminds me of the time we lined smudge pots up and
down the rows of groves to keep the freeze from killing
the crop, and of how I welcomed my first kiss one evening
in the crook of the arm of one of those fragrant trees.

Because the moon was full and teasing the tide with her
shimmer when I caught a striped schoolmaster at midnight
even though the fish weren't biting on our side of the party
boat, and you scaled and fileted my keeper on the dock,
packed the pink flesh in ice for the ride home, and I cooked
it with lemon and butter and wine, and with our fingers,
we fed the perfect flaky morsels to each other's mouths.

—ELISA ALBO

Menudo

INGREDIENTS

Mezcal	Bay Leaves
Stars	Garlic
Tripe	Onion
Copal	Chiles Guajillos
Hen	Limes
Dogs	Salt
Cow's Feet	Coffee
Narrow Bones	Tepito
Oregano	Tortillas

DIRECTIONS

1. When your macho comes home gurgling a bottle of mezcal, begin the menudo.
2. He'll whisper: *Te amo chiquitita,* then palm your face to the window. You'll scan for stars made invisible by streetlamps & whisper: *Stars see.* He'll let go & laugh: *I've never liked Estrellita.*
3. When he falls asleep at your feet, remember: he is un buen macho.
4. Cut tripe into ribbons in the sink. Finger curved ridges clean. Tripe: though combed it is a bowel.
5. Light copal in a warm clay bowl until it melts to sap. Make the sign of the cross on your lips; grit its ash against your teeth.
6. In a large pot: tripe, cow's feet, narrow bones, onion, oregano, garlic & salt. Add cold water & simmer all night.
7. Go to bed. Ignore the smell of shit; it will linger in the house for days.
8. Rise with the rooster & ring a hen's neck. Drain the hen of its blood; hold its clucking still so it doesn't wake your macho. Hang on a hook.
9. Drain the broth of boiled blood w/ a funnel & a tight mesh sieve. Pull any meat from their bones & throw cartilage to the dogs hungry on the patio.

10. Clean chiles of membranes, roast on comal. Turn each chile soft in a pot of hot water, then grind. Wash your hands with oil made from the rind of a lime.
11. Combine & let simmer: broth, chiles, tripe, bay leaves.
12. In a bowl: limes. In a shaker: oregano. Both: on the table. The table: floats. Hold it down by fists & a ladle.
13. Wake your macho: provide coffee, provide tepito.
14. Watch him eat. Your kitchen will grow a film of fat you must clean, the tortillas hard in their wait.
15. *You look tired*, he'll say. *You look worse*, you'll say. Nod & know he'll be home from work late. Pluck feathers from your hanged hen in the yard.

—NATALIE SCENTERS-ZAPICO

Ode to the Avocado

Oh fickle pod, some days you are too hard,
an unyielding block of sun-cured clay,
surly and thick of will, inedible.
Some days you are too soft, a pliant mash,
spineless, and splintered with rot.
Oh toad-fist nugget, green-meated heart,
pimpled and dimpled, glazed organ
of modest fuel, purse of nutrients,
let me love my fickle self as I love you,
cursed though we are by these imperfect
margins, this cycling life with its humble
center and changeable flesh,
this too brief and faultless peak.

—MELISSA DICKSON

Duck Confit

4:06 a.m., late July, two blue feet bare
on carpet in a refrigerated bedroom,
is no time to ponder class prerogatives.
Nor is 4:08, kitchen bulbs lengthening doorways,
appropriate to reflect upon effete habits,
or decades of your mother risen in the dark
to tent a bloated November bird in foil
and heat while the house slept, by god, soundly.
4:11 I can assure you is no time for indulgence,
for silliness, to rethink life's bargain.
It is the moment, instead, glasses askew,
to lift each thigh from overnight caress
of garlic, fresh bay leaf, home-harvested thyme,
to massage flesh under cold water
with priestly certainty, free all excess of salt,
lay each upon its pallet of skin and fat.
4:15, moreover, is time for concubine
to administer olive oil bath, up to the top
and one quarter inch more for decadent measure,
four cups of green virgin, first-press,
sampled from drowsy fingertips to drowsy lips.
Priest, concubine, virgin? 4:17 subdued to 200°,
think merely some thought of this sort:
14 hours remain between toil and ascendance.
The creaking hinge of a dual-oven stove,
a door raised to closure. An expectant silence.
4:19, however, dog's distant wheeze
unheard from your master bed, blazing day to come
still only suspicion behind any woods
looked to for solace, 4:19, when one may lower
a switch and night commence its imponderable
strategy—that's another story altogether.
Think then what you will, once work is done.
And sleep again, sweet prince, if you're able.

—GAYLORD BREWER

Why I Can't Cook for Your Self-Centered Architect Cousin

Because to me a dinner table's like a bed—
without love, it's all appetite and stains. Let's buy
take-out for your cousin, or order pizza—his toppings—

but I can't lift a spatula to serve him what I am.
Instead, invite our favorite misfits over: I'll feed
shaggy Otis who, after filet mignon, raised his plate

and sipped merlot sauce with such pleasure
my ego pardoned his manners. Or I'll call Mimi,
the chubby librarian, who paused over tiramisu—

"I haven't felt so satisfied since . . ." then cried
into its curls of chocolate. Or Randolph might stop by,
who once, celebrating his breakup with the vegetarian,

so packed the purse seine of his wiry body with shrimp
he unbuttoned his jeans and spent the evening
couched, "waiting for the swelling to go down."

Or maybe I'll just cook for us. I'll crush pine nuts
unhinged from the cones' prickly shingles.
I'll whittle the parmesan, and if I grate a knuckle

it's just more of me in my cooking. I'll disrobe
garlic cloves of rosy sheaths, thresh the basil
till moist, and liberate the oil. Then I'll dance

that green joy through the fettuccine, a tumbling,
leggy dish we'll imitate, after dessert.
If my embrace detects the five pounds you win

each year, you will merely seem a generous
portion. And if you bring my hand to your lips
and smell the garlic that lingers, that scents

the sweat you lick from the hollows of my clavicles,
you're tasting the reason that I can't cook
for your cousin—my saucy, my strongly seasoned love.

—BETH ANN FENNELLY

Pesach in Blacksburg

is ushered in by the neighborhood Easter egg
hunt, my kids scrambling beneath backyard
playsets for chocolate, by the ads I've been
seeing on Facebook for weeks for the Messianic

Jews welcoming Yeshua at the local Holiday Inn—
is matzo that comes in giant bulk multipacks
of six stacked on an end-cap shelf at the Kroger,
though each of the few Jewish families in town

only needs a single box or maybe two, and someone
(a stockboy?) has hung a neat row of Fried Pork Skins
nestled against the Manischwitz Matzo Ball Soup Mix,
the Kedem sparkling grape juice, and gefilte fish slabs

suspended in glass jars. Pesach in Blacksburg is a
complication, an exile, and we are the small but
holy remnant, so we open the door during Seder
for Elijah the Prophet to find a neighbor selling

magazine subscriptions for a Young Life fundraiser.
We welcome the stranger, but I'm sure this is not
what the Haggadah meant when it says, *Let all
who are hungry come and eat,* and this year

again we defrost the shankbone Jenny left
before she moved to Baltimore, and this year
the kids wear plague masks I ordered from
amazon.com (hail, lice, locusts, boils, fire,

and a few others, though I still find the closed
eyes on the Slaying of the First Born unbearable),
and this year again only some of us know the songs,
but we sing them over and over: *Dayenu,* if He had

supplied our needs in the desert for forty years,
it would have been enough—and the kids eke out
a weak Four Questions with the help of the adults,
then ransack the house for the Afikomen. This is a

shadow of the Seders of my youth, the lace table
cloths, my survivor grandfather in his resplendent
satin robe at the table's head leading, switching
between Hebrew and Yiddish, but we do what

we can, so I string together folding tables in the
dining room and guests roll in with wine and extra
chairs, and here is the bread of affliction, of far-
from-home, of galut, that we eat and eat and eat.

—ERIKA MEITNER

Married

Tonight I ask my husband to help me remember
names for the breeds of chickens
he and I grew up with, living on neighboring farms.
From the far, tall grasses he calls them:
    Wyandottes. Dominiques. Barred Rocks.
    Rhode Island Reds. Silver Spangled Hamburgs.
    Leghorns. Anconas. Buff Orpingtons . . .
"Mother used to call them 'Buff Orphans,'" I interrupt.
We laugh. He remembers my mother.
Evening settles itself,
whispering snow.
The kitchen nightlight makes a tiny moon
on the wall.

     —JO McDOUGALL

Easy

We ask each day what you're hungry for,
try Loretta's roast, some chicken, corn
and peas. A few bites, you're through, unless
we say there's cake. Mom kept ice cream
in the hospital fridge; now everyone brings
things we know you'll eat—Betty's coconut
pie or Ronda's lemon icebox, Aunt Elaine's
strawberry cake (its icing a thick sludge
of butter, strawberries, sugar, cream cheese).
Uncle Ken drops by with fried pies
from M.J.'s, says he knows you like the peach.

When the apples we'd overbought were going
bad, Suzanne stopped by with a recipe for easy
apple dumplings and stuff to make it, crescent
rolls, sugar, a can of Mountain Dew—
Mom pops the top, pours it over
the whole pan of wrapped and sugared apples,
when she's through, slides it in the oven.

On TV we see people losing homes,
roads closed, rivers flooding, a tornado
somewhere, near—the local news, but elsewhere
a royal wedding, froth of gown and gossip.
My first day back, you asked about *your mate*,
referred to Romans 1, but now we've settled
into something new—not easy, but less
of all that stuff about choice and sin,
the how and when of why we didn't talk
for so long back then. I sit beside the bed,
we eat apple dumplings, watch TV,
saying nothing, just eating something easy.

—ED MADDEN

A Theory of Pole Beans

(for Ethel and Rice)

that must have been the tail end of the Depression
as well as the depression of coming war
there certainly was segregation and hatred and fear

these small towns and small minded people
trying to bend taller spirits down
were unable to succeed

there couldn't have been too much fun
assuming fun equates with irresponsibility

there was always food to be put on the table
clothes to be washed and ironed
hair to be pressed
gardens to be weeded

and children to talk to and teach
each other to love
and tend to

pole beans are not everyone's favorite
they make you think of pieces of fat back
cornbread
and maybe a piece of fried chicken

they are the staples of things unquestioned
they are broken and boiled

no one would say life handed you
a silver spoon or golden parachute
but you still
met   married
bought a home   reared a family
supported a church   and kept a mighty faith
in your God   and each other

they say love/is a many splendored thing
but maybe that's because we recognize
you loved no matter what the burden
you laughed no matter for the tears
you persevered in your love

and your garden remains in full bloom

—NIKKI GIOVANNI

Because Men Do What They Want to Do

and we do what has to be done. That's
what *that's* about, Aunt Gwen said. My arms heavy with corn

for shucking. The sink filled with plucked greens for
cleaning. Aunt Ethel, arms akimbo, hands in bright yellow

gloves just nodded in my direction before she tended
the collards again. And I'll tell you what else—Aunt Dot

had been silent; we all paused as she punctuated her chopping
with words—Yes, get the plate when he asks you. String up the linens,

turn down the beds. But once in a while, pick up a plate,
like so. Throw it down. Oh yes, said Aunt Bebe, leaning

out to the screen porch, blowing smoke out of doors.
Frequency may vary. The kitchen erupted. While the

men had been cheering the football game in the parlor,
the laughter tipped the house—every ear fled a body,

collected against that kitchen's closed door. Bebe flicked out
her cigarette, rinsed her hands, went back to breaking up chickens.

Ethel furiously scrubbed the greens. Gwen, to the boiling
potatoes on the stove and Dot, her chopping. Too new to know better,

J—my husband—peered around the door then darted out. I
grinned with teeth, tore at the silk. *Yes,* Ethel whispered. *Just like that.*

Show him any old hand can make a fist.

—TJ JARRETT

Sleeping Like Silverware

Ten weeks
we slept like silverware.

No, not silverware in the drawer.
Not like forks,
stem cradled to stem,
tines aligned formally with tines.
Not like butter knives,
passive and parallel,
butt to butt
and blade to blade.
And certainly nothing at all like spoons,
snug and complacent
in their curved receptacles.

The way we slept,
if we slept at all,
was more like silverware
in the dishwasher
at the end of the economy cycle.

Jostled by steamed water,
tangled,
knives with forks with spoons,
the odd spatula or ladle,
ensnarled in the white
squares of the basket,
blasted clean,
still damp,
and a little too hot to sort out.

—Devon Brenner

After Grandma Novi's Recipe for Blackberry Cake
Is Lost at the Press and There's No Place Left to Look

I take a notion to look up for it, into the evening sky.
I don't know any gods or goddesses, so I will say
that to the east, where night has stained darkest
is where she drained the berries. I'll say those four
high stars set like cornerstones are the table where she worked,
and that low, roundish cluster of near and far stars
is the gleam of berries in her bowl. To the west,
where the sky is still light, is how the cake rose
while we waited with our plates.
                                    That long gray tail
of cloud near the horizon is how she loosed from hairpins
the knot of a single long braid and combed it with her fingers
before she went to bed that night. There, where the sky
just begins to bruise, is how she sighed.

—DIANE GILLIAM

Eating a Muffaletta in Des Moines

Don't do it
even if you've never had one before
unless you come by my house
on a Sunday afternoon probably
in summer when I'm not teaching
because that's when I'll have time.

I'm not saying I'm inviting you over. Just saying
that around here they'll give you something
with olives and ham and Swiss on a
goddamn garlic focaccia,
quarter it, wrap it in plastic
and call it a muffaletta sandwich.
It's probably got some Cajun seasoning
in there too because people not from
New Orleans who've maybe been to
New Orleans on vacation and think they know
New Orleans as a result call
New Orleans "Cajun country"
and put Tabasco on everything
and talk about how terrible Katrina was
and how drunk they got on Bourbon Street
that time at Mardi Gras
and if they yell "Hey la-bas!"
in front of me they might
just get knocked the fuck out
that's all I'm saying.

Garlic focaccia is a fine bread,
don't get me wrong
but it's not muffaletta.
It's good for soaking up olive oil with
a little cracked pepper or balsamic.
I'm not a barbarian.

But a muffaletta needs crunch
in the crust, like you're breaking
through years to get to the meat
and the olives and the pepper
and that bread better not be
falling apart like your first marriage
did after her crying confession
on I-12 West that she was cheating
and her name was Alexis and you said
what like from Dynasty? and the leaky AC
dripped ice cold condensation all over
your right foot and you were glad
it was over even tho it took
a year for it to be over-over
and you had to cover court costs with
an unsubsidized student loan check
that you're still paying on to this day.
No soggy first marriage bread is what
I'm saying. Second marriage bread,
sturdy, takes-no-shit-from-you bread,
tells the salami and ham and provolone
and most of all that giardinera
(spicy for me but I'll take it easy on you)
to know their place
in the goddamn universe.

You can't get that bread here.
You really can't get it anywhere
but in New Orleans because
it's not the kind of loaf you can use
for anything else, and who needs
a sandwich like this more than
a couple three times a year?
You'd die if you ate it more
than that. So somebody visits
New Orleans and wanders out
of Central Grocery with one

and needs it a year later
and there's no bread to make it
so they wind up with this bullshit
soggy soft bread with some mortadella
and boiled ham and baby Swiss and a handful
of pimento-stuffed manzanilla olives
and goddamn it no one should live like that.
Come by my house. I'll make the bread.

—BRIAN SPEARS

Salt

for Veedra
(Miami, Florida)

Allergic to fish (shellfish or otherwise)
my sister shouts *Watermelon!*
when surprised by a fruit dinner
at the resort where she and I are sharing
sister time, something we rarely do.
I am old enough to be her aunt, or
even her mother. Fifteen years older
in fact, and like a mother, I take delight
in her delight. She won't be hungry
this evening, the chef has prepared
something especially for her, having
no idea what she looks like, only that
a temporary resident needs something
beyond seafood. Only the fruit is untainted.
A gentleman from Georgia sits with us
as we wait on our dinner. He, from "a good family"
"strong values" "can go back several generations"
looks at me, directly into my black pupils, and
I know what he knows. A whole history rides
the vehicle, the mule train, the wagon, the dust
track of my sister's outburst. And we begin
to laugh, hysterically. He for all the expected
reasons. And I, I laugh because somewhere
I want to cry. The landscape under my breasts,
topography of pines, clay bottomland, roofs
of tin . . . and the lie of it. The fruit so sweet, so
red, and now seedless. He and I both know
how delicious such things can be, but he can eat his
without shame, without notice.

And my sister in all her Yankee naïveté, or
innocence, knows only that she is being served
a treat, something that won't swell her throat,
noose her breath, while he and I share
our secret through grins, giggling
until we damn near choke.

—VIEVEE FRANCIS

The Gospel of Barbecue

for Alvester James

Long after it was
necessary, Uncle
Vess ate the leavings
off the hog, doused
them with vinegar sauce.
He ate chewy abominations.
Then came high pressure.
Then came the little pills.
Then came the doctor
who stole Vess's second
sight, the predication
of pig's blood every
fourth Sunday.
Then came the stillness
of barn earth, no more
trembling at his step.
Then came the end
of the rib, but before
his eyes clouded,
Uncle Vess wrote
down the gospel
of barbecue.

Chapter one:
Somebody got to die
with something at some
time or another.

Chapter two:
Don't ever trust
white folk to cook
your meat until
it's done to the bone.

Chapter three:
December is the best
time for hog killing.
The meat won't
spoil as quick.
Screams and blood
freeze over before
they hit the air.

Chapter four, Verse one:
Great Grandma Mandy
used to say food
you was whipped
for tasted the best.

Chapter four, Verse two:
Old Master knew to lock
the ham bacon chops
away quick or the slaves
would rob him blind.
He knew a padlock
to the smokehouse
was best to prevent
stealing, but even the
sorriest of slaves would
risk a beating for a full
belly. So Christmas time
he give his nasty
leftovers to the well
behaved. The head ears
snout tail fatback
chitlins feet ribs balls.
He thought gratitude
made a good seasoning.

Chapter five:
Unclean means dirty
means filthy means
underwear worn too
long in summertime heat.
Perfectly good food
can't be no sin.
Maybe the little
bit of meat on ribs
makes for lean eating.
Maybe the pink flesh
is tasteless until you add
onions garlic black
pepper tomatoes
soured apple cider
but survival ain't never been
no crime against nature
or Maker. See, stay alive
in the meantime, laugh
a little harder. Go on
and gnaw that bone clean.

—HONORÉE FANONNE JEFFERS

Grace

Because my grandmother made me
the breakfast her mother made her,
when I crack the eggs, pat the butter
on the toast, and remember the bacon
to cast iron, to fork, to plate, to tongue,
my great grandmother moves my hands
to whisk, to spatula, to biscuit ring,
and I move her hands too, making
her mess, so the syllable of batter
I'll find tomorrow beneath the fridge
and the strew of salt and oil are all
memorials, like the pan-fried chicken
that whistles in the grease in the voice
of my best friend's grandmother
like a midnight mockingbird,
and the smoke from the grill
is the smell of my father coming home
from the furnace and the tang
of vinegar and char is the smell
of Birmingham, the smell
of coming home, of history, redolent
as the salt of black-and-white film
when I unwrap the sandwich
from the wax-paper the wax-paper
crackling like the cold grass
along the Selma to Montgomery road,
like the foil that held
Medgar's last meal, a square of tin
that is just the ghost of that barbecue
I can imagine to my tongue
when I stand at the pit with my brother
and think of all the hands and mouths
and breaths of air that sharpened
this flavor and handed it down to us,
I feel all those hands inside

my hands when it's time to spread
the table linen or lift a coffin rail
and when the smoke billows from the pit
I think of my uncle, I think of my uncle
rising, not falling, when I raise
the buttermilk and the cornmeal to the light
before giving them to the skillet
and sometimes I say the recipe
to the air and sometimes I say his name
or her name or her name
and sometimes I just set the table
because meals are memorials
that teach us how to move,
history moves in us as we raise
our voices and then our glasses
to pour a little out for those
who poured out everything for us,
we pour ourselves for them,
so they can eat again.

—JAKE ADAM YORK

Contributor Notes

ELISA ALBO was born in Havana and grew up in Lakeland, Florida, eating Cuban, Spanish, Turkish, and Southern food. Her chapbooks are *Passage to America* and *Each Day More*. Her poetry has appeared in *Alimentum*, *Irrepressible Appetites*, *Notre Dame Review*, *Potomac*, and *Two-Countries Anthology*. At Broward College, she teaches English and ESL, including a popular themed course, Food in Film and Literature. She lives with her husband and daughters in Plantation, Florida.

ELIZABETH ALEXANDER is a poet, essayist, and professor. In addition to editing various collections of writing, she is the author of six books of poems, two collections of essays, a play, and a memoir, *The Light of the World*. She is president of the Andrew W. Mellon Foundation, as well as a chancellor of the Academy of American Poets, and the Wun Tsun Tam Mellon Professor of the Humanities at Columbia University. She previously served as the inaugural Frederick Iseman Professor of Poetry at Yale University, where she chaired the African American Studies Department. In 2009, she composed and delivered "Praise Song for the Day" for the inauguration of President Barack Obama.

SHIRLETTE AMMONS is an associate producer for the Emmy and Peabody Award–winning docuseries *A Chef's Life*, which is in its fifth season and airs on PBS stations throughout the country. She is also a writer and musician whose body of work includes two poetry collections, three music projects, and numerous collaborations. Ammons is a Cave Canem Fellow, an alumna of the Next Level Program—an international hip-hop diplomacy program of the U.S. Embassy and UNC's Music Department, where she taught hip-hop lyricism in Belgrade and Novi Sad, Serbia—as well as a recipient of the North Carolina Arts Council Artist Fellowship Award. Ammons resides in Durham, North Carolina.

RICHARD BLANCO is the fifth presidential inaugural poet in U.S. history—the youngest and first Latino and gay person to serve in such a role. Born in Madrid to Cuban exile parents and raised in Miami, he centers his poetry collections and memoirs on the negotiation of cultural identity. Blanco's many awards include the Agnes Lynch Starrett Poetry Prize, the PEN Beyond Margins Award, the Paterson Poetry Prize, and a Lambda Literary Award. He is a Woodrow Wilson Fellow and the education ambassador at the Academy of American Poets.

DEVON BRENNER transplanted from Michigan to Mississippi in 1999. She is a professor of literacy education at Mississippi State University, where she works with local schools to increase the time students spend reading and writing.

GAYLORD BREWER is a professor at Middle Tennessee State University, where he founded and for more than twenty years edited the journal *Poems & Plays*. His most recent books are the cookbook-memoir *The Poet's Guide to Food, Drink, & Desire* and a tenth collection of poetry, *The Feral Condition*. He delivered the invocation at the eleventh SFA Symposium in 2008.

JERICHO BROWN is the recipient of fellowships from the John Simon Guggenheim Foundation, the Radcliffe Institute for Advanced Study at Harvard University, and the National Endowment for the Arts. His poems have appeared in the *New York Times* and the *New Yorker*. His first book, *Please*, won the American Book Award. His second book, *The New Testament*, won the Anisfield-Wolf Book Award. He is an associate professor at Emory University and poetry editor for *The Believer*.

MOLLY McCULLY BROWN is the author of *The Virginia State Colony for Epileptics and Feebleminded*, which won the 2016 Lexi Rudnitsky First Book Prize. Her poems and essays have appeared in *Gulf Coast*, *Ninth Letter*, *Pleiades*, *Image*, *Colorado Review*, and elsewhere. In 2017–18, she lived and worked in Little Rock, Arkansas, as the inaugural Jeff Baskin Writers Fellow at *Oxford American* magazine.

NICKOLE BROWN's books include *Sister* and *Fanny Says* and the chapbook *To Those Who Were Our First Gods*. She was the editorial assistant for the late Hunter S. Thompson, worked at Sarabande Books for ten years, and was an assistant professor at the University of Arkansas at Little Rock. Currently, she is the editor for the Marie Alexander Poetry Series and lives with her wife, poet Jessica Jacobs, in Asheville, North Carolina. Because she'll always be Fanny's granddaughter and was raised in Kentucky, there's nothing she loves better in the morning than a fresh Pepsi, and she puts Frank's RedHot on damn near everything except ice cream.

GREG BROWNDERVILLE is the author of *A Horse with Holes in It*, *Deep Down in the Delta*, and *Gust*. At Southern Methodist University in Dallas, he serves as associate professor of English, director of creative writing, and editor in chief of the *Southwest Review*.

GABRIELLE CALVOCORESSI is the author of three collections: *Rocket Fantastic*, *Apocalyptic Swing*, and *The Last Time I Saw Amelia Earhart*. Her poems have been featured in *American Poetry Review*, *Boston Review*, the *New York Times*, and the *Washington Post*. She is assistant professor and Walker Percy Fellow in Poetry at the University of North Carolina at Chapel Hill.

WO CHAN is a poet and drag performer. Chan holds honors from Kundiman, Lambda Literary, and the Asian American Writers' Workshop and is the author of the chaplet *Order the World, Mom*. Wo Chan has performed work at NY Live Art, Dixon Place, BAM Fisher, and National Sawdust. Chan is currently an MFA candidate in poetry at NYU.

MELISSA DICKSON is the author of two poetry collections: *Cameo* and *Sweet Aegis: Medusa Poems*. She is the coeditor of *Stone, River, Sky*, an anthology of Georgia poems from Negative Capability Press. Her work has appeared in *Shenandoah*, *Southern Humanities Review*, *North American Review*, *The Bitter Southerner*, *Southern Womens' Review*, *Gravy*, and *Cumberland River Review*. A mother of four, she also teaches at the University of West Georgia.

JOHN T. EDGE has served as director since the 1999 founding of the Southern Foodways Alliance, an institute of the Center for the Study of Southern Culture at the University of Mississippi. Winner of the M. F. K. Fisher Distinguished Writing Award from the James Beard Foundation, he is the author of *The Potlikker Papers: A Food History of the Modern South*, published by Penguin in 2017. He holds an MA in Southern studies from the University of Mississippi and an MFA in creative nonfiction from Goucher College.

KELLY NORMAN ELLIS is an associate professor of English and creative writing at Chicago State University. Chair of the Department of English, Foreign Languages, and Literatures and director of the MFA in Creative Writing Program at CSU, she has published two poetry collections, *Tougaloo Blues* and *Offerings of Desire*.

W. RALPH EUBANKS is the author of *Ever Is a Long Time: A Journey into Mississippi's Dark Past* and *The House at the End of the Road: The Story of Three Generations of an Interracial Family in the American South*. His essays and criticism have appeared in the *Washington Post*, the *Wall Street Journal*, the *American Scholar*, *Wired*, and the *New Yorker*, as well as on NPR. A 2007 Guggenheim Fellow, he is currently a visiting professor of English and Southern studies at the University of Mississippi.

BETH ANN FENNELLY, the poet laureate of Mississippi, teaches in the MFA Program at the University of Mississippi, where she was named Outstanding Teacher of the Year. She has won grants from the National Endowment for the Arts and United States Artists and a Fulbright to Brazil. Her sixth book, *Heating & Cooling: 52 Micro-Memoirs*, was recently published by W. W. Norton.

NIKKY FINNEY was born in South Carolina and raised during the civil rights, black power, and black arts movements. She is the author of four books of poetry, *On Wings Made of Gauze*, *RICE*, *The World Is Round*, and *Head Off & Split*, which won the National Book Award for Poetry in 2011. She holds the John H. Bennett, Jr., Chair in Creative Writing and Southern Letters at the University of South Carolina in Columbia.

VIEVEE FRANCIS, who is Texan, is the author of three books of poetry: *Blue-Tail Fly*, *Horse in the Dark*, and *Forest Primeval*. She is the recipient of the Hurston Wright Legacy Award and the Kingsley-Tufts Poetry Award. Her work has appeared in numerous publications including *Poetry*; the *Best American Poetry* anthologies of 2010, 2014, and 2017; and *Angles of Ascent: A Norton Anthology of Contemporary African American Poetry*. She serves as an associate editor for *Callaloo*.

DIANE GILLIAM is the author of *Dreadful Wind & Rain*, *Kettle Bottom*, *One of Everything*, and *Recipe for Blackberry Cake* (chapbook). She is the most recent recipient of the Gift of Freedom from the A Room of Her Own Foundation.

NIKKI GIOVANNI was born in Knoxville, Tennessee, in 1943. Since 1987 she has been on the faculty at Virginia Tech, where she is a University Distinguished Professor. She writes: A long time ago a little girl sat in the window of the bedroom she shared with her older sister and read by finger flashlight. She looked at the stars when the battery gave way, and when she got older, she snuggled under her grandmother's quilts to listen all night to jazz on the radio—or at least until she fell asleep. She first fell in love with words, then they somehow seemed to fall in love with her. She got to learn history, meet people, travel everywhere, and since this is a good fairy tale, she lives happily ever after. There may be other things along the way, but the words and the stars and the music are all that matter.

ELTON GLASER, a native of New Orleans, is Distinguished Professor Emeritus of English at the University of Akron, where he also directed the University of Akron Press and edited the Akron Series in Poetry. Glaser has published eight full-length collections of poetry, most recently *The Law of Falling Bodies* and *Translations from the Flesh*.

SEAN HILL is the author of *Dangerous Goods,* winner of a Minnesota Book Award, and *Blood Ties & Brown Liquor,* named one of ten "Books All Georgians Should Read" in 2015. His poems have appeared in *Callaloo, Harvard Review, Poetry, Tin House,* and numerous other journals and anthologies. He has received fellowships and awards from many organizations and institutions including Cave Canem, Bread Loaf, the University of Wisconsin–Madison, Stanford University, and the National Endowment for the Arts.

JAY HOPLER's most recent book of poetry, *The Abridged History of Rainfall,* was a finalist for the 2016 National Book Award in Poetry. He teaches in the writing program at the University of South Florida.

REBECCA GAYLE HOWELL is the author of *American Purgatory* and *Render /An Apocalypse* and the translator of Amal al-Jubouri's verse memoir of the Iraq War, *Hagar before the Occupation / Hagar after the Occupation*; since 2014 she has edited poetry for *Oxford American.* Howell lives with her family in Knott County, Kentucky, where she serves as the James Still Writer-in-Residence at the Hindman Settlement School.

TJ JARRETT is a writer and software developer in Nashville, Tennessee. Her recent work has been published in *Poetry Magazine, African American Review, Boston Review, Beloit Poetry Journal, Callaloo, VQR,* and other periodicals. She has been anthologized in *Language Lessons* by Third Man Books and *Best American Non-Required Reading 2015* from Houghton-Mifflin. Her debut collection, *Ain't No Grave,* was published by New Issues Press, and her second collection, *Zion* (winner of the 2013 Crab Orchard Open Competition), was published by Southern Illinois University Press.

HONORÉE FANONNE JEFFERS is a poet, fiction writer, literary and cultural critic, and the author of four books of poetry: *The Gospel of Barbecue, Outlandish Blues, Red Clay Suite,* and *The Glory Gets.* A native southerner, Jeffers now lives on the prairie where she has taught creative writing since 2002. She is a full professor of English at the University of Oklahoma.

ASHLEY M. JONES earned an MFA in Poetry from Florida International University, where she was a John S. and James L. Knight Fellow. Her work is published or forthcoming in *Academy of American Poets, Tupelo Quarterly, Obsidian,* and many other journals and anthologies. She won a 2015 Rona Jaffe Foundation Writer's Award, and her debut collection, *Magic City Gospel,* won the Silver Medal in Poetry in the 2017 Independent Publishers Book Awards.

GEORGE ELLA LYON is originally from Harlan County, Kentucky. Her recent books include *Many-Storied House: Poems*; *Boats Float!*, cowritten with her son Benn, and *Voices from the March on Washington*, cowritten with J. Patrick Lewis. The author of "Where I'm From," Lyon served as Kentucky poet laureate (2015–16). For more information, visit www.georgeellalyon.com.

ED MADDEN is the author of four books of poetry, most recently *Ark*. His poems have appeared in *Crazyhorse*, *Prairie Schooner*, and other journals, as well as in *Best New Poets 2007* and *Hard Lines: Rough South Poetry*. In 2015, he was named the poet laureate for the city of Columbia, South Carolina.

JO MCDOUGALL has published seven books of poetry and a memoir, *Daddy's Money: A Memoir of Farm and Family*. The University of Arkansas Press published her collected poems, *In the Home of the Famous Dead*, in 2015. She has received awards from the Readers Digest / DeWitt Wallace Foundation, the Academy of American Poets, the Arkansas Arts Council, and the Porter Prize Foundation of Arkansas, as well as multiple fellowships from the MacDowell Colony. She has been inducted into the Arkansas Writers' Hall of Fame. A native of the Arkansas delta, she now resides in Little Rock. She was recently appointed the poet laureate of Arkansas.

MICHAEL MCFEE is the author of eleven books of poetry, most recently *We Were Once Here*. His second collection of essays, *Appointed Rounds*, was published by Mercer University Press in 2018. A native of Asheville, North Carolina, he received the James Still Award for Writing about the Appalachian South from the Fellowship of Southern Writers. McFee teaches in the creative writing program at UNC–Chapel Hill.

ROSE MCLARNEY's collections of poems are *Its Day Being Gone*, winner of the 2013 National Poetry Series, published by Penguin Books, and *The Always Broken Plates of Mountains*, published by Four Way Books. McLarney is an associate professor at Auburn University and co-editor of the *Southern Humanities Review*, as well as the forthcoming anthology *A Literary Field Guide to Southern Appalachia*. The poem "Vocabulary Lesson" was prompted by Allison Burkette's article on "The Cornbread Question," which appeared in the winter 2015–16 issue of *Gravy*.

ERIKA MEITNER is the author of five books of poetry, including *Ideal Cities*, which was a 2009 National Poetry Series winner, *Copia*, and *Holy Moly Carry Me*. She is an associate professor of English at Virginia Tech, where she directs the undergraduate and MFA programs in creative writing.

ROBERT MORGAN is the author of fifteen books of poems, most recently *Terroir* and *Dark Energy*. He has published eleven works of fiction, including *Chasing the North Star* and *As Rain Turns to Snow*. Nonfiction works include *Boone: A Biography* and *Lions of the West*. A member of the Fellowship of Southern Writers and a native of western North Carolina, he is currently Kappa Alpha Professor of English at Cornell University.

NAOMI SHIHAB NYE lives in old downtown San Antonio, Texas, under towering pecan trees a block from the river. Her most recent books are *The Turtle of Oman*, a novel for elementary readers, and *Famous*, a picture book illustrated by Lisa Desimini.

JON PINEDA's poetry collection *Little Anodynes* won the 2016 Library of Virginia Literary Award for Poetry. His new novel, *Let's No One Get Hurt*, was published in 2018 by Farrar, Straus and Giroux.

IAIN HALEY POLLOCK's debut collection of poems, *Spit Back a Boy*, won the 2010 Cave Canem Poetry Prize. His new work is scheduled to appear in *African American Review*, *American Poetry Review*, and *Poetry Northwest*. Pollock teaches at Rye Country Day School in Rye, New York, and at the Solstice MFA Program of Pine Manor College in Chestnut Hill, Massachusetts.

LYNN POWELL's most recent book of poetry is *Season of the Second Thought*, winner of the Felix Pollak Prize from the University of Wisconsin Press. She has published two previous books of poetry—*Old & New Testaments* and *The Zones of Paradise*—and a book of nonfiction, *Framing Innocence*. A native of East Tennessee, Powell now lives in Oberlin, Ohio, where she teaches in the creative writing program of Oberlin College.

ATSURO RILEY was brought up in the South Carolina lowcountry. He is the author of *Romey's Order*, winner of the Kate Tufts Discovery Award, the Whiting Writers' Award, the Believer Poetry Award, and the Witter Bynner Fellowship from the Library of Congress. His work has been honored with fellowships from the Lannan Foundation and the NEA and anthologized in *Poems of the American South*, *The Open Door: One Hundred Poems, One Hundred Years of Poetry Magazine*, and *The Oxford Anthology of Contemporary American Poetry*.

ILIANA ROCHA earned her PhD in English literature and creative writing from Western Michigan University. Her work has been featured in the *Best New Poets 2014* anthology, as well as *Bennington Review*, *Blackbird*, and *West Branch*. *Karankawa*, her debut collection, won the 2014 AWP Donald Hall Prize for Poetry and is available through the University of Pittsburgh Press.

NATALIE SCENTERS-ZAPICO is the author of *The Verging Cities*, winner of the PEN / Joyce Osterweil Award, the GLCA Award, the Utah Book Award, and the NACCS Book Award. Her second book, *Lima :: Limón*, is forthcoming from Copper Canyon Press.

JULIE SOLA, in addition to her work as a fine artist with many shows over the years in the Middle Tennessee area, is the author of two locally successful children's books, *Run Fast Milo* and *Possum Dreams*. Sola is the producer of Proto-Pulp: Classic Books of the Future, an annual children's book fair held at the Idea Hatchery, also in East Nashville. For more information, visit www.fatcrowpress.com.

BRIAN SPEARS is the author of *A Witness in Exile* and the senior poetry editor of the *Rumpus*. He lives and writes in Des Moines, far from the New Orleans suburbs where he learned to cook and eat.

SHERYL ST. GERMAIN has published four full-length poetry books, two chapbooks, and three collections of linked essays, including *Fifty Miles*, forthcoming from Etruscan Press in 2019. *The Small Door of Your Death*, a collection of poems about the death of her son, appeared with Autumn House Press in 2018. A native of New Orleans, she directs the MFA program in creative writing at Chatham University.

GARLAND STROTHER, a native of Tensas Parish, Louisiana, is a retired librarian now living near New Orleans. His work has been published in the *Texas Review*, *Arkansas Review*, and other journals, as well as in *The Southern Poetry Anthology*.

ADRIENNE SU is the author of four books of poems, most recently *Living Quarters*, and the recipient of a 2007 NEA fellowship. Born and raised in Atlanta, she studied at Harvard and Radcliffe Colleges and the University of Virginia. At Dickinson College, in Carlisle, Pennsylvania, she teaches in the creative writing and food studies programs.

SARAH LOUDIN THOMAS grew up on a one-hundred-acre farm in French Creek, West Virginia, the seventh generation to live there. Her award-winning Christian fiction is set primarily in West Virginia and celebrates the people, the land, and the heritage of Appalachia. Her fourth novel, *The Sound of Rain*, was released in November 2017. Sarah and her husband, Jim, live in the mountains of western North Carolina.

NATASHA TRETHEWEY served two terms as the nineteenth poet laureate of the United States (2012–14) and a term as poet laureate of the state of Mississippi (2012–16). She is the author of four collections of poetry: *Domestic Work*, *Bellocq's Ophelia*, *Native Guard*, for which she was awarded the 2007 Pulitzer Prize, and most recently, *Thrall*. Her book of creative nonfiction, *Beyond Katrina: A Meditation on the Mississippi Gulf Coast*, was published in 2010. A fellow of the American Academy of Arts and Sciences, she is Board of Trustees Professor of English at Northwestern University.

JON TRIBBLE is the author of two collections of poems: *Natural State* and *And There Is Many a Good Thing*. His third book, *God of the Kitchen*, is forthcoming from Glass Lyre Press in 2018. He is the managing editor of *Crab Orchard Review* and the series editor of the Crab Orchard Series in Poetry, published by SIU Press.

ADAM VINES is an associate professor of English at the University of Alabama at Birmingham, where he is the editor of *Birmingham Poetry Review*. He is the author of *Out of Speech* and *The Coal Life* and coauthor, with Allen Jih, of *Day Kink* and *According to Discretion*.

FRANK X WALKER, former Kentucky poet laureate, is a founder of the Affrilachian Poets and the author of eight collections of poetry including *Turn Me Loose: The Unghosting of Medgar Evers*. Voted one of the most creative professors in the South, he is the originator of the word "Affrilachia." The Lannan Poetry Fellowship Award recipient has degrees from Spalding University and University of Kentucky, were he serves as a professor in the Department of English and the African American and Africana Studies Program.

CAROLINE RANDALL WILLIAMS, a native of Nashville, Tennessee, is a cookbook author, young adult novelist, and poet. She received her MFA from the University of Mississippi and is currently writer in residence at Fisk University. She has been named by *Southern Living* magazine as one of "50 People Changing the South." February 2015 saw the publication of *Soul Food Love*, a cookbook written by Randall Williams and her mother, the novelist Alice Randall, that goes beyond basic recipes to cover the past, present, and future of a misunderstood cuisine. Her poetry has appeared in several journals, including *Iowa Review*, *Massachusetts Review*, and *Palimpsest*. Her debut poetry collection, *Lucy Negro, Redux*, came out in 2015 from Ampersand Books.

L. LAMAR WILSON is the author of *Sacrilegion* and coauthor of *Prime: Poetry and Conversation*, with the Phantastique Five. He's a recipient of fellowships from the Cave Canem Foundation, the Callaloo Workshops, and the Blyden and Roberta Jackson Fund at the University of North Carolina at Chapel Hill, where he earned his doctorate in African American and multiethnic American poetics. Wilson, an Affrilachian Poet, teaches creative writing and African American literature at the University of Alabama.

SYLVIA WOODS, a native of Kentucky, is a former English teacher who lives in Oak Ridge, Tennessee. Her work has appeared in many anthologies and literary journals, including *Appalachian Heritage*, *Motif*, and *The Southern Poetry Anthology*. She is working on a collection of poems about language.

MARIANNE WORTHINGTON is a poet, editor, and educator who cofounded *Still: The Journal* (www.stilljournal.net) in 2009, an online literary magazine dedicated to publishing writers, artists, and musicians with ties to the Appalachian region. She received the Al Smith Fellowship from the Kentucky Arts Council, the Artist Enrichment Grant from the Kentucky Foundation for Women, and the Appalachian Book of the Year Award for her poetry collection, *Larger Bodies Than Mine*. She lives in southeastern Kentucky.

JAKE ADAM YORK authored four books of poems: *Murder Ballads*, *A Murmuration of Starlings*, *Persons Unknown*, and *Abide*, which was published posthumously. He served as a visiting faculty fellow at the James Weldon Johnson Institute for Advanced Study at Emory University (2011–12). He was also a recipient of a fellowship from the National Endowment for the Arts. At the time of his death in 2012, he was an associate professor of English at the University of Colorado Denver and edited the journal *Copper Nickel*.

KEVIN YOUNG is the director of the Schomburg Center for Research in Black Culture. He is the author of thirteen books, most recently *Brown*; *Blue Laws: Selected & Uncollected Poems 1995–2015*, longlisted for the National Book Award; and *Book of Hours*, winner of the Lenore Marshall Prize from the Academy of American Poets. Young's nonfiction book *The Grey Album: On the Blackness of Blackness* won the Graywolf Press Nonfiction Prize and the PEN Open Book Award. His most recent nonfiction book is *Bunk: The Rise of Hoaxes, Humbug, Plagiarists, Phonies, Post-Facts, and Fake News*, winner of the Anisfield-Wolf Book Award in Nonfiction. He is the editor of eight collections, including *The Collected Poems of Lucille Clifton, 1965–2010* and *The Hungry Ear: Poems of Food and Drink*. Young was inducted into the American Academy of Arts and Sciences in 2016. He serves as poetry editor of the *New Yorker*.

Permissions and Credits

"Why It's Delicious," from *Passage to America*, copyright 2016 by Elisa Albo, Main Street Rag Publishing Company.

"Talk Radio, D.C.," from *Body of Life*, copyright 1996 by Elizabeth Alexander, Tia Chucha Press.

"Food Stamps," copyright 2018 by Shirlette Ammons.

"Mango, Number 61," from *City of a Hundred Fires*, by Richard Blanco, © 1998. Reprinted by permission of the University of Pittsburgh Press.

"Sleeping Like Silverware" first published by *Inkwell*, copyright 2018 by Devon Brenner.

"Duck Confit," from *The Martini Diet*, copyright 2008 by Gaylord Brewer, Dream Horse Press.

"Like Father," from *Please*, copyright 2008 by Jericho Brown, New Issues Poetry and Prose.

"When My Mother Is Away," copyright 2018 by Molly McCully Brown.

"Fanny Says How to Make Potato Salad," from *Fanny Says*. Copyright © 2015 by Nickole Brown. Reprinted with the permission of the Permissions Company, Inc., on behalf of BOA Editions, Ltd., www.boaeditions.org.

"Carlo Flunks the Seventh Grade" from *Gust*. Copyright © 2011 by Greg Alan Brownderville. Published 2011 by Tri Quarterly Books/ Northwestern University Press. All rights reserved.

"Jubilee," from *Apocalyptic Swing*. Copyright © 2012 by Gabrielle Calvocoressi. Reprinted with the permission of Persea Books, New York. All rights reserved.

"such as," first published by *AAWW / The Margins*, copyright 2018 by Wo Chan.

"Ode to the Avocado," first published by *Graze*, copyright 2018 by Melissa Dickson.

"Cook," copyright 2018 by Kelly Norman Ellis.

"Why I Can't Cook for Your Self-Centered Architect Cousin," from *Open House*, by Beth Ann Fennelly. Copyright 2002 by Beth Ann Fennelly. Used by permission of W. W. Norton & Company, Inc.

"Liberty Street Seafood," from *Head Off & Split*. Copyright © 2011 by Nikky Finney. Published 2011 by Tri Quarterly Books/Northwestern University Press. All rights reserved.

"Salt," from *Forest Primeval*. Copyright © 2016 by Vievee Francis. Published 2016 by Tri Quarterly Books/Northwestern University Press. All rights reserved.

About the Editor

SANDRA BEASLEY is the author of *Count the Waves*; *I Was the Jukebox*, winner of the 2009 Barnard Women Poets Prize; and *Theories of Falling*, winner of the 2007 New Issues Poetry Prize. She is also the author of *Don't Kill the Birthday Girl: Tales from an Allergic Life*, a disability memoir and cultural history of food allergy.

Honors for her work include a 2015 Literature Fellowship from the National Endowment for the Arts, the 2015 C. P. Cavafy Prize from *Poetry International*, the 2013 Center for Book Arts Chapbook Prize, and the 2008 Maureen Egen Exchange Award from *Poets & Writers*. She has held distinguished writer residencies at Wichita State University, Cornell College, Lenoir-Rhyne University, and the University of Mississippi, and she was a featured author for the 2013–14 Georgia Poetry Circuit. She has received three Artist Fellowships and two Larry Neal Writers' Awards from the D.C. Commission on the Arts and Humanities in support of her writing. She has also been awarded fellowships to the Sewanee Writers' Conference, the Hermitage Artist Retreat, the Jentel Artist Residency, the Millay Colony, the Vermont Studio Center, and the Virginia Center for Creative Arts.

Her poetry has appeared in numerous journals including *Gravy*, *Poetry*, *Virginia Quarterly Review*, *Tin House*, and *Gulf Coast*. She has been in a number of anthologies, including the 2010 edition of *The Best American Poetry*. Her prose has appeared in such venues as the *New York Times*, the *Washington Post*, and *Oxford American*.

A native of Virginia, Beasley has lived in Washington, D.C., for many years. She teaches as part of the University of Tampa's low-residency MFA program.

About the Southern Foodways Alliance

The Southern Foodways Alliance, founded in 1999, documents, studies, and explores the diverse food cultures of the changing American South.

Our work sets a welcome table where all may consider our history and our future in a spirit of respect and reconciliation.

A member-supported organization based at the University of Mississippi's Center for the Study of Southern Culture, we collect oral histories, produce films, sponsor scholarship, mentor students, stage events, and publish *Gravy*, a journal of great writing and a biweekly podcast. Donations from generous individuals, foundations, and companies fund our work. The SFA showcases a South that is constantly evolving. Our work complicates stereotypes, documents new dynamics, and gives voice to the often unsung folk who grow, cook, and serve our daily meals.

For more information, please visit www.southernfoodways.org.